Open your heart –
Manifest your dreams

Nichiren Buddhism 4.2

**Susanne Matsudo-Kiliani
and Yukio Matsudo**

COPYRIGHT AND DISCLAIMER

© 2023 Yukio Matsudo & Susanne Matsudo-Kiliani

This edition was published in October 2023 by DPI Publishing, Heidelberg, Germany.

All rights reserved. No part of this publication may be reproduced by any mechanical, photographic or electronic process, or in the form of phonographic recording; nor may it be stored in a retrieval system, transmitted or otherwise be copied for public or private use, other than for 'fair use' as brief quotations embodied in articles and reviews, without prior permission in writing of the author.

The information given in this book should not be treated as a substitute for professional therapeutic or medical advice. Any use of information in this book is at the reader's discretion and risk. Neither the author nor the publisher can be held responsible for any loss, claim or damage arising out of use, or misuse, of the suggestions made, the failure to take therapeutic or medical advice or for any material on third party websites.

ISBN: 979-8871402276

Contents

Foreword	**7**

Chapter 1
It is the heart that matters — 10

We can change the world with our heart	15
Body and mind influence each other	*17*
Case study 1	*17*
The emotional basis of stress	*18*
Your body is your subconscious mind	*19*
Disease is mainly caused by emotional stress	*19*
Your believing heart decides the quality of your life	20
What does "faith" really mean?	*20*
Nichiren encourages us to dream big	*23*
Exercise 1	*26*

Chapter 2
The power of the heart — 27

Heart intelligence	27
Your heart remembers well	*28*
Your authentic memories are in your heart	*29*
Case study 2	*30*
The electromagnetic field of the heart	31
Energy field in the body	*31*
Your heart´s energy field	*31*
Case study 3	*32*
Electromagnetic fields generated by the heart	*33*
Exercise 2	*35*
The heart is more powerful than the brain	36
The heart sends out your state of life!	38
Trinity of mind, body, and heart	38

Chapter 3
Heart coherence and Heart Rate Variability — 41

The believing heart refers to a pure heart	41
What is coherence?	**42**

Heart Rate and Heart Rate Variability 44
A marker for longevity and biological aging 47
The nervous systems of our body 48
The Sympathetic and the Parasympathetic Nervous System 49
We need both functions well-coordinated! 50
HRV is an indicator of your ANS balance 51
The global health crisis of chronic diseases 52
The limits of conventional medicine 54
The effects of an ANS imbalance 56
Comparing an exhausted and an energetic person 58

Chapter 4
HRV analysis of Daimoku 61

Comparison of HRV changes in four cases 61
HRV parameters 62
SDNN 62
pNN50 64
RMSSD 65
Stress index 67
Total Power 68
You will grow younger 69

Chapter 5
The power of Heart Coherence 71

The heart is your emotional center 71
Coherent or incoherent heart rhythm 72
Your brain responds to the rhythm of your heart 73
Your emotions determine your energy 74
Positive emotions lead to a coherent heart rhythm 74
Exercise 3 76

Coherence has an uplifting effect on others 76
Coherence is the underlying physical condition of the flow state 78
Emotions that drain our energy 79
Exercise 4 80

Our state of life is a physiological baseline 81
Our state of life acts like a thermostat 82
The amygdala reacts to our heart rhythm 83
Exercise 5: What emotions do you keep falling back into? 84
You cannot change your baseline with your mind 85

way you will understand deeply why and how to open your heart to manifest your dreams.

This book is written primarily from the perspective of Susanne Matsudo-Kiliani, with Yukio Matsudo as co-author contributing his deep and extensive knowledge of Nichiren Buddhism.

We would like to deeply thank Lisa Kossoff, Enrique Fernández and Steve Bell for their extraordinary help in proofreading and editing the English version of this book. We would also like to thank Traecy Berryman for the wonderful work in designing the book cover with great grace and artistry, as well as for the many presentation images for our workshops.

Susanne Matsudo-Kiliani and Yukio Matsudo

Chapter 1
It is the heart that matters

> If we never challenge the impossible, we will never know the true power of chanting Nam-myoho-renge-kyo.
> — *Daisaku Ikeda*

It was a cold winter week in December 2018. Everybody was getting in the mood for Christmas shopping, having a hot wine at the Christmas market and putting on some candles at home. Three weeks before Christmas Eve I woke up early as my mobile phone had been ringing. I ignored it, because I thought this was just one of these advertisement calls I got the week before. Later, however, I just had a very quick look at the message on the mobile phone and saw that Michael had been sending me a message. Michael is the husband of my friend Astrid. I wondered why he and not Astrid had contacted me directly if she wanted to tell me something. I quickly opened his message and could not believe what I was reading. He wrote me that Astrid had had a brain hemorrhage and had been immediately delivered to the emergency unit of the university clinic.

The doctor in charge had first put her in an artificial coma to operate her on her head. However, the attempt to wake her up from the artificial coma had failed and now she had fallen into a natural coma. The doctors had told him that this was not a good sign and that "she was in a very critical situation and that things did not look good." Thus, Michael sent this SMS to me asking whether we could chant Daimoku for his wife.

This was the first time that he took our practice serious. Though he did not mind that Astrid had been practicing Nichiren friend could not make it and my environment seemed to constantly confirm this thought. But my heart desperately wanted her to be alive and healthy. I am happy that in this case my heart won over my head.

We can change the world with our heart

> What kind of future do I envision for myself? What kind of self am I trying to develop? What do I want to accomplish in my life? The thing is to paint this vision of your life *in your heart* as specifically as possible. The power of the heart enables us to actually create with our lives a wonderful masterpiece in accordance with that design. — Daisaku Ikeda

In our modern age, scientists have searched for the seat of consciousness primarily by examining the functions of the brain. However, modern scientists like cardiologist Pim van Lommel, are questioning whether the brain is the only seat of consciousness. In fact, many ancient traditions thought of the heart as the primary seat of consciousness; as the key to accessing our inner wisdom. In many ancient cultures, the heart was considered to be more important than the brain. Likewise, Nichiren regarded the "contemplation of one's own heart"

(*Kanjin*) as the centerpiece of his practice and regarded the heart as *"the most important"* in our daily practice.

Again, he is backed up by modern science. For new research shows that the human heart is much more than just an efficient pump that sustains life. The heart is a physical structure performing an essential function in your body, not only circulating your blood, but also creating hormones and beating out a rhythm that informs and regulates every aspect of your body. The heart is actually the center of your energetic system, it is the most powerful source of electromagnetic energy in the human body, powering your physical heart and body, and also giving rise to your emotions.

The heart is also the core of yourself: your inner source; your connection to the Infinite, your true authentic self and the ultimate embodiment of all that you are and all that you become in your life.

New findings suggest the heart is also an access point to a source of wisdom, love and intelligence which enables us to manifest our goals and attain greater emotional balance, enhanced creativity and heightened intuitive capacities. All of these aspects are important for increasing personal effectiveness, improving your health and relationships and achieving greater fulfillment.

Nichiren recognized more than 750 years ago that the heart is the seat of emotions and exerts a decisive influence on its own environment. He tells us to live from the heart. This enabled me to understand that we need to connect to the heart as our center rather than our brain. For he strongly emphasized the motto:[1]

> Become the master of your heart instead of letting your heart rule you!

This refers to the purification and transformation of negative thoughts and emotions, which is an indispensable prerequisite for creating your reality in a positive way, as we shall see later on.

And once again science is beginning to reveal evidence that supports what Nichiren knew all along. There is fascinating research that is orientating us back to our heart as a

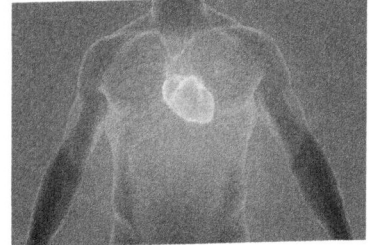

In fact, as a Buddhist scholar and practitioner, Nichiren was familiar with both our negative life tendencies laden with karma, and the limitations of our mental control of life. He knew that willpower alone was not enough to change our life. Thus, he used to emphasize *"faith"* and the need *"to strengthen our faith"*. In one of his letters, Nichiren makes an analogy comparing our dark nature to the dark night and the Lotus Sutra to the moon.

> Within the minds of all human beings, there exist the three categories of illusions of thought and desire, [...] as well as karma created by the ten evil acts or the five cardinal sins — all of which are like a dark night. The Flower Garland and the other various sutras are like stars in this dark night, while the Lotus Sutra is like the moon. For those who have faith in the Lotus Sutra, but whose faith is not deep, it is as though a half-moon were lighting the darkness. But for those who have profound faith, it is as though a full moon were illuminating the night.
> *The essence of the "Medicine King" Chapter*, WND I, p.94

This analogy with the moon at night, highlights the importance of the intensity of the light of the moon, which represents the depth of faith. But what does Nichiren mean by *"profound faith"*? How can we deepen and strengthen our faith?

When Nichiren used to encourage his followers to "muster their faith", he seemingly had a very clear understanding of the primacy of the heart over the mind or brain function.

> It is the heart that really matters. No matter how earnestly Nichiren prays for you, if you lack faith, it will be like trying to set fire to wet tinder. Spur yourself to muster the power of faith. [...] Employ the strategy of the Lotus Sutra before any other.
> *The Strategy of the Lotus Sutra (Reply to Shijō Kingo)*, WND I, p.1001-2

However, I have often asked myself, "What does it mean to have faith in the Buddhist practice?" "Isn't it enough to believe in the power of Daimoku and the Gohonzon?"[7] "Am I not practicing a strong belief when I chant Daimoku with great determination and concentration?"

Until I understood the primacy of emotions and feeling in the practice of Daimoku, the term "faith" (*shin*) had been a very abstract concept to me, and I could not really grasp it until, as mentioned above, I realized that Nichiren actually uses the terms *"believing heart"* or *"faith in your heart"* (*shinjin*) in the same way. Only since I understood the connection to emotions and feelings, could I make sense of the term "faith". It was something you could *feel* and not *think about*. After changing my focus from my mind to my heart, reading the following passage made me happy in the knowledge that my emotions were a reality switch; the key to changing my life.

> As for the "believing heart" (*shinjin*), there is nothing unusual. It means to chant Nam-myoho-renge-kyo placing one's faith in the Lotus Sutra, Shakyamuni, [...,] and benevolent deities, just as a woman cherishes her husband, while a man lays down his life for his wife, as parents refuse to abandon their children, or as a child keeps attached to its mother.
> The Meaning of Faith
> (Reply to the lay nun Myōichi), WND I, p.1036

Nichiren's reference to the "believing heart" gave me the opportunity to make a paradigm shift in my Buddhist practice from a head-centered to a heart-focused practice. To love and to enjoy chanting Daimoku was the key.

Setting a clear goal is the first step in achieving it.
Your intention then needs to be accompanied
by a joyful and positive emotion in your heart.

Nichiren encourages us to dream big

Nichiren often uses the term "heart" (*kokoro*) as synonym for "faith" (*shin*) but also in the sense of "believing heart" (*shinjin*). In this context, *Shin-jin* also means "opening up your heart" to many new possibilities in your life, based on self-confidence and optimistic belief. You are deeply convinced that everything will turn out fine, even if the situation you find yourself in looks difficult or even impossible from a "rational" point of view or from what is commonly considered "possible". It means to go beyond any conventional concepts and familiar beliefs. To take a leap in faith or as our American friend Steve Bell would put it: "*To have faith means to not worry about the outcome anymore and to feel that things will turn out fine.*"

I have often heard some people say, "*Buddhism is reasonable,*" suggesting that one should think and act in a rational and acceptable manner, in accordance with what is generally considered to be normal and "realistic". This approach emphasizes your own personal effort and willpower, because it does not accept anything magical or miraculous beyond your daily reality and ego consciousness. I have often wondered if and how people can change their life situation, if they chant with such a limited mindset. In contrast, I myself have experienced and heard of so many "wonderful", "miraculous" stories that were only possible in collaboration with something greater than our own willpower and ego-consciousness.

Now, let's take a look at the Japanese original text related to the statement on "reasonable Buddhist teaching."

> Unhardened iron melts quickly in a blazing fire, like ice in hot water. But a sword can withstand the heat for a while even when exposed to a large fire because it is well forged. [...] Buddhism is *reason (dōri)*. Reason will win over your lord.
> *The Hero of the World*, WND I, p. 1169 / p.839

The Japanese term "*dōri*" stands for a "reasonable principle" or "reasonable principles" related to various aspects such as an ethical code, logical consistency and a natural law. As in this letter, Nichiren often applies natural phenomena to our daily situation to explain that Buddhist causality is more fundamental than any secular regulation. When comparing this term to a natural law, Nichiren tells us that the power of Daimoku is as powerful and unfolds as compellingly as a natural law. Just like a magnet attracts iron filings, for example. In the case of an ethical code, this means that if your employer, boss or even your friend acts in a humiliating or even degrading way towards you, you can change the situation for the better, because according to Nichiren the spiritual dimension of Daimoku is much more powerful than any secular law or regulation. Nichiren tells us that we can overcome a worldly conflict with the power of Daimoku, for example if we have been treated unfairly. This was proven by Shijo Kingo, a well-known protector and follower of Nichiren Daishonin, who was punished by his lord by having part of his land taken away. But later, Shijo Kingo got twice as much land back. Nichiren himself was sentenced to death but one just could not kill him.

Therefore, the translated statement that "*Buddhism is reason*" has nothing to do with the misunderstood idea that we should act or think in a reasonable, rational, normal and realistic or even mediocre way. On the contrary, Nichiren teaches that the effect of Daimoku is powerful and compelling like the laws of nature, like a magnet that attracts iron filings, like birds flying in synchrony, and like our personal experiences of synchronicity.

Believing that chanting Daimoku only means to act in a reasonable way, however, makes many people remain within the conventional framework of "normality" and what is normally considered to be "possible". This way you don´t dare to dream big anymore or to believe in "miracles".

In contrast, nature is full of wonders and miracles and contains a deep mystical aspect. Thus, Nichiren even encourages us to go beyond any boundaries of our individual, social and cultural worldview, which often tells us to think "normally and soberly." In fact, if we just want to experience normal possibilities, we don't need the practice of Daimoku.

> Don't be realistic, because all you are doing is limiting what is possible for you to experience. Challenge yourself to stay true to your own heart and believe in a new possibility! You can have a dream and make the seemingly impossible possible.

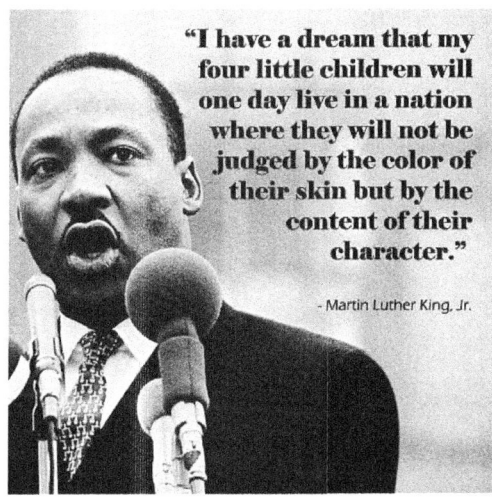

"I have a dream that my four little children will one day live in a nation where they will not be judged by the color of their skin but by the content of their character."

- Martin Luther King, Jr.

In this sense, Nichiren encourages us to dream our biggest dream when chanting Daimoku. If you do not have dreams anymore, you will lose your passion and limit yourself to the reality you have known up to now. Martin Luther King said "I have a dream". He did not say " I have a goal". If you do not expect change, change will never happen. In dreaming big, however, you will have to confront that voice within you that starts doubting your dream and tells you "what if…" this is not possible or all nonsense? Or what if I go for my dream and fail? Or what if I am too old for this? Or my energy is too low? I am sure you know many other doubts and worries that can come up. If you are not careful these doubtful voices can sabotage your dreams with their ever- so reasonable objections. However, this is actually an opportunity to deepen your commitment and conviction to your dream. It is also an opportunity to find out more about your internal limiting beliefs and to overcome them. It is possible. Those three words are at the core of your dream come true.

Exercise 1

Are you more committed to your current reality or to the future of your dreams?

What are you doing to move that dream forward?

Chapter 2
The power of the heart

> Everyone has an amazing gift to bring forward. The heart space is the source of this genius. Going towards the middle of the heart is going towards the stillness that connects us all and where all information is present. From there, the brain and the intellect can interpret and apply it in a beautiful way... The heart is the fundamental space for our evolution. The heart is the place from which our society will transcend our current difficulties. – *Nassim Haramein*

Heart intelligence

For centuries, we thought that the brain was the body's main organ while the heart was considered merely a physical pump. However, Nichiren tells us that the heart is not only the master organ of the body but also our connection to feelings, emotions and to our Higher Selves. Most important it is our connection to an innate intelligence. Again, he is backed up by modern science.

Our heart is more than just a muscle pump.

The new sciences, and particularly the advanced research of the specialist in this field, the HeartMath Institute in California, are recognizing the true significance of the heart as a source that generates electromagnetic fields and as our connection to non-local consciousness. That being said, it turns out that the heart is actually the center of emotions and memories. But more importantly, the heart is the primary organ in our body. It even has its own "brain" and its own way of storing memories. It produces hormones, and it is a powerful signal generator in our bodies. Above all, it is more powerful than the brain.

Your heart remembers well

Our journey to the heart takes us deeper into the body, into the center of our being. We no longer think of the heart as just a muscle that pumps blood through our body. We are now aware that the heart is more like the brain than any other organ in the body.

In 1991, a breakthrough in relation to the heart showed that our memories are not only stored in our brains. Scientists have found that there are specialized cells in every human heart. And that was something really unexpected. Your heart has about 40,000 specialized cells called sensory neurites. They are essentially brain-like cells, but they are not in your brain, only in your heart. However, they are so closely networked that they are actually called the little brain in the heart. They think, feel and remember independently of the brain.[8]

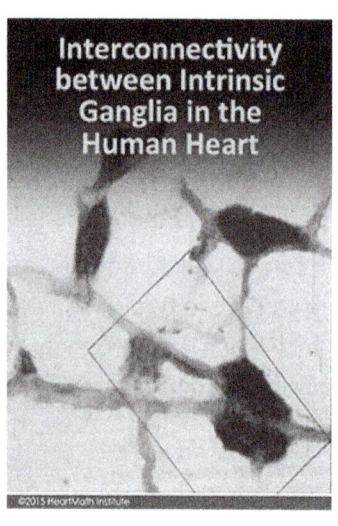

Interconnectivity between Intrinsic Ganglia in the Human Heart

In fact, some scientists believe the heart could even function semi-independently as its own neural network. Due to these specialized cells in the heart, scientists are now saying that the heart literally has its own brain. This allows the heart to learn, remember, even to feel and sense independently of the brain. Think about what that means! When you have an experience in your life that is profound and has a strong emotional impact on you, how can you transform it, so that it does not impact you again and again? If it's a joyful experience, it usually doesn't pose a problem. But it starts to get painful when we're hurt: when we're betrayed by people we trust, or when we experience a loss.

For years I thought that we could solve this pain by processing it with our mind. By talking about it and analyzing the experience. I have seen many people try to overcome their past experiences in this way, and after a while I realized that it doesn't necessarily change the emotional charge of past experiences. Just the memory of my parents' illnesses or their deaths; just the memory of friends and relatives who abandoned or disappointed me, evoked the same response. I became depressed and felt as if I was experiencing the same pain again. Those feelings were still stored in my body and would surface at unexpected times when something triggered them. I had to dig deeper. I learnt that we need to transform the old wounds in our hearts, not only in our minds.

But how do we transform the memories and the hurtful emotions stored in the heart's sensory neurites? Because remember, these neurites learn: they remember the experiences; they feel and sense them. That means when we talk about *heart intelligence* - when we talk about *memory in our heart* - it's not just a metaphor. It is a literal memory that remains in the heart, even when the heart is no longer in the original body where the experiences were made.

Your authentic memories are in your heart

There are many stories of heart transplant patients who developed different food cravings or tastes in music or altered personality traits after the transplant.

One woman who used to love classical music suddenly developed a surprising liking for rock music, motorcycles and fast food after a heart transplant. It turned out that she had received the heart of a 19-year-old man who had died in a motorcycle accident.

Dr. Paul Pearsall, Clinical Professor at the Hawaii University Department of Nursing, has researched the transmission of memories through organ transplantation. He has conducted extensive interviews with nearly 150 heart and other organ transplant recipients, including their families or friends and the families or friends of the donor. Among other things, he published a study presenting ten significant cases that show *"changes in heart transplant recipients that parallel the personalities of their donors."*[9]

In one case, an 18-year-old boy who wrote poetry, played music and composed songs, died in a car accident. A year after his death, his parents came across a cassette tape of a song he had written, called, *Danny, My Heart is Yours*, which was about how he "*felt he was destined to die and give his heart to someone.*" His heart donor recipient "Danny" was an 18-year-old girl named Danielle. When she met the donor's parents, they played some of his music and she was able to complete the phrases, even though she had never heard the song,

Case study 2

> The most fascinating case study is that of an eight-year-old girl who received the heart of a murdered ten-year-old girl. It was a successful transplant and immediately the eight-year-old girl began having vivid nightmares and reoccurring memories of being murdered. The girl´s mother took her to a psychiatrist who was convinced that the girl was dreaming about events that had really occurred.
> They contacted the police and the girl described in such detail what happened in her dreams that night and what she saw. She gave such detailed information including the time and the place of the murder and the specific words said to her by the man who had chased her. The girl was able to

Did you know that your heart emits an electromagnetic field that changes according to your emotional state – and that others can perceive the quality of your emotions through the electromagnetic energy emanating from your heart? We always communicate with each other on the energetic level through our hearts.[10] That means:

> Our thoughts and emotions affect the magnetic field of the heart, which has an energetic effect on our environment, whether we are aware of it or not.

Over the past 15 years, the HeartMath Institute has shown that our deepest beliefs, convictions and feelings are transmitted in electromagnetic waves through our hearts, to the environment. When we have a feeling in our hearts, we are creating electrical and magnetic waves inside of our bodies that extend beyond our bodies into the world around us.

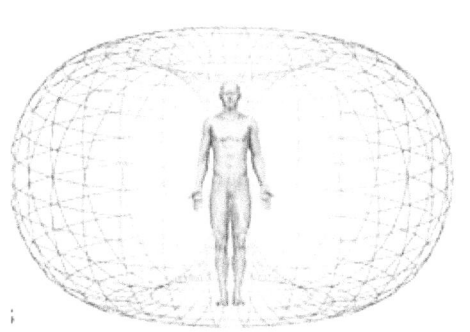

You may also have experienced the strange phenomenon of *cardio-electromagnetic communication* when you have just met or been talking to someone and suddenly you feel uplifted, excited or even depressed. This has happened to me on many occasions. Let´s give you an example.

Case study 3

> I made friends with a really nice and kind woman. However, whenever I met her alone and enjoyed our conversation, it

describe in detail what this man looked like. Based on the drawing made by the authorities and all the details she provided, they quickly found a man who matched the description in a small town in the American Midwest. He broke down and admitted killing the eight-year-old girl. He was convicted and sentenced and is in prison based on the memories of a heart from the person whose life he took. That's how real these memories are in your heart.

So, if you've been struggling with certain emotional issues and have tried to solve them with your mind or through conversation, this is only half the story. It's not complete. The rest of the story is in your heart.

The electromagnetic field of the heart

Energy field in the body

When I started chanting, I began to feel some emotional relief from certain memories. It was like gradually lowering the volume of these emotions.

According to meditational researcher Dr. Joe Dispenza, these memories are also stored in the electromagnetic field that surrounds the cells of the heart. Each cell is surrounded by an invisible energy field that gives life to that cell. An organ also has an invisible field of electromagnetic energy. This organ actually receives information from that invisible energy field. According to Dispenza, the memory of the organ actually exists in this electromagnetic field. This can impact heart transplant patients in some fascinating ways.

Your heart´s energy field

However, it is not just your inner scenery and environment that is controlled by these heart memories. They also affect your external environment.

wasn't until afterwards that I noticed my energy level had dropped terribly. I often felt exhausted and depressed for a few days. Meeting her really drained my energy. In this way, I realized that I needed to pay more attention to both the emotional and energetic aspects in my life.

I could never explain this phenomenon until I realized that being near the electromagnetic field of a person's heart puts you in resonance with the person's feelings and beliefs. I knew she was frustrated and depressed about her life. Every time I talked to her I could deeply feel this state of life. You can pretend you're having a good time. However, your heart's electromagnetic field tells others exactly how you're feeling.

Electromagnetic fields generated by the heart

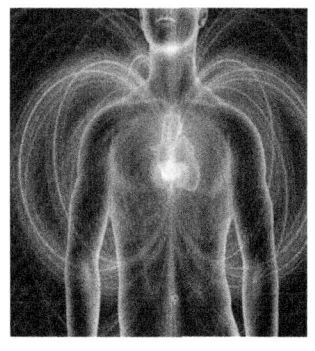

The HeartMath Institute solved this puzzle by discovering that psychophysiological information can be encoded into the electromagnetic fields generated by the heart.

Research shows that those electromagnetic waves of the heart extend not just one meter or two meters, but many kilometers from where your heart physically resides.

The heart's electromagnetic field radiates your emotions. With this we also strongly influence our environment, particularly when people stand close together or touch each other.

The results of these experiments have shown that the nervous system acts as an antenna, which is tuned to and responds to the magnetic fields produced by the hearts of other individuals. That's why feelings can be contagious. This kind of exchange is called *energetic information exchange*. Furthermore, it has been observed that this energetic communication ability can be enhanced, resulting in a much deeper level of non-verbal communication, understanding and connection between people.

Research by the HeartMath Institute has also shown that when two people meet, the current brain waves of one person register the heart rate and information of the other person and get in resonance with them.

Our thoughts and emotions affect the heart´s magnetic field, which energetically affects our environment whether or not we are conscious of it.

In this way, we are constantly communicating with the outside world, sharing our deepest emotions and attitudes without even saying a word.

The example below shows two different power spectra based on some electrocardiogram (ECG) data recorded during two different psychophysiological modes: *appreciation* and *anger*.

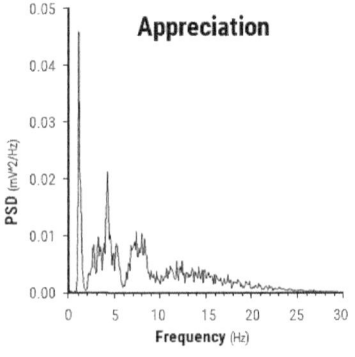
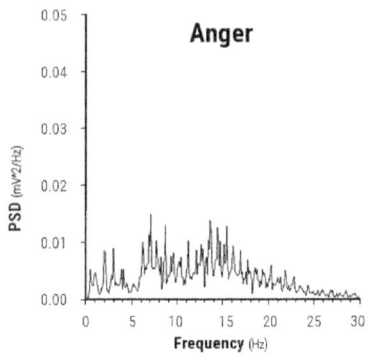

The above graphs indicate there is a direct relationship between the heart rhythm patterns and the spectral information encoded in the magnetic field emitted by the heart. This information about a person's emotional state is communicated throughout the body and into the external environment.[11] Different emotions literally put you in a different frequency.

> Our heart is a kind of transformer that is converting all our beliefs and emotions into electrical and magnetic vibrations.

However, your radiance changes when you chant. My experience is that when I chant, I purify and transform my emotions on the deepest level, and this becomes also evident on the exterior level. I have often noticed that people have a clearer and more positive vibe after chanting Daimoku for half an hour or an hour.

Other people react differently to me, depending on whether I have chanted before or not. Our state of life is shared non-verbally. According to the HeartMath Institute, we send out all of our programming and deep-seated beliefs as information in the form of emotions that are emitted into our environment as electromagnetic waves.

Exercise 2

Can you feel and observe how contagious emotions are?

_____

Do you feel some specifically strong energy in the presence of certain people in your environment?

A. _____

B. _____

C. _____

Can you observe a change in their vibrations after chanting Daimoku?

_____

How do you affect your environment with your emotions?

_____

The heart is more powerful than the brain

Our thoughts and feelings are energetic in nature, with thoughts producing electrical energy. This was clearly shown in the measurements of the brainwave frequencies during our Daimoku meditation which we described in our book "Change your brainwaves- change your karma – Nichiren Buddhism 3.1". An even stronger effect, however, comes from our feelings which we send out through our hearts. The research of the HeartMath Institute confirms:

> The electromagnetic field generated by the heart represents the largest and most powerful rhythmic electromagnetic field generated by the body.

This field around your body touches everything around it. This also means that you influence every single person you have a relationship with. Research has shown that when your signal is coherent and strong, it has a positive effect on the autonomic nervous systems of those around you. This means that we cannot hide our state of being. Because in this field, our deepest emotions and convictions are encoded and thereby transmitted to the outside world.

The research of the HeartMath Institute provided another surprise. In 2003, Dr. Rollin McCraty used an ECG machine and

The heart sends out your state of life!

> The quantum field does not respond to what you want, but to who you are being. Dr. Joe Dispenza

According to Dr. Joe Dispenza, the thoughts we think are sending electrical signals to our environment and the feelings that accompany those thoughts, attract events to our life in a magnetic way which enables us to experience even more of this particular emotion. This means that if we constantly feel worried, frustrated or abandoned, we continue to feel worried, frustrated or abandoned in the future. Fear generates more fear; frustration generates more frustration. However, the contrary is also true. Feeling loved, appreciated, abundant, empowered and joyful generates more love, appreciation, abundance, empowerment and joy in our lives. We have to break our karmic cycle by transforming and changing our emotions. This is why chanting Daimoku is such a powerful pattern breaker.

Trinity of mind, body, and heart

At this point, given the important role of the heart and emotions, it is neither sufficient nor correct to just talk about "*the oneness or non-duality of body and mind*". This usual English translation of the Nichiren Buddhist principle of *Shikishin-funi* does not take into account the emotions, which are directly related to the heart. This principle acts not only as a bridge connecting the mental function of the mind with the physiological function of the body, but also as a hidden

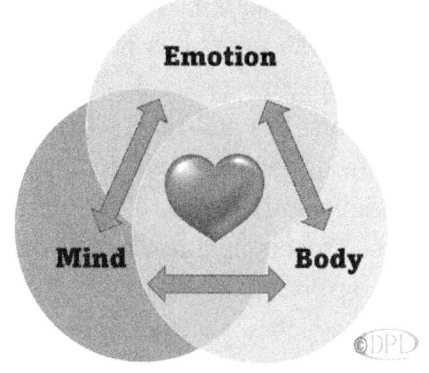

other heart monitors to measure the amplitude of brain waves versus heart waves. While the brain does have an electrical and a magnetic field, they are both relatively weak compared to those of the heart. He discovered that the electrical field of the heart is 100 times stronger than the electrical field of the brain. What was really sensational however, was his discovery that the magnetic field produced by the heart was about 5.000 times more powerful than the magnetic field produced by the brain. This means that the heart is about a hundred times stronger electrically, and up to 5,000 times stronger magnetically, than the brain.

> The magnetic field of the heart is 5000 times stronger than the magnetic field of the brain.

And these energy changes are based on your *feelings*; not your thoughts. So, it doesn't matter if you convince your mind logically, that you can have something or want something. *If your heart doesn't believe it, it will never manifest.*

This also means that when you're happy for no particular reason, you become a magnet for what you desire! When you loosen up on the outcome and focus on feeling good, good things come naturally to you. You no longer rely on getting something or somewhere to feel good.

For, our hearts send our inner states of life to the outside world - with enormous power. These emitted vibrations then resonate with events and situations that correspond to that life-condition. This also means that no matter how hard you try to manifest wealth and love, for instance, you will always hit an insurmountable barrier, if your heart is burdened with unprocessed resentment and negative energies. If you do not let go of past disappointments and the heavy emotions associated with them, they will block your ability to manifest your dreams.

center of power and control that provides mind and body with energy and information. Therefore, we would like to revise our understanding of this Buddhist principle into a threefold relationship of mind, body and emotion.

> The principle of *Shikishin-funi* means: On the one hand, the mind and the body have their own specific functions. On the other hand, these two different domains are connected through the emotions that are directly related to the heart. This principle should not only be understood as the non-duality of mind and body, but as *the trinity of mind, body and heart*. The heart refers to the energetic dimension which is also inherent in our lives.

This concept of the trinity of mind, body and emotion corresponds to the multilayer model of Dr. Watkins, as introduced in Chapter 1 of our previous book NB4.1 (see picture below). In parallel, we remind you of a different approach to understanding the complex mechanism of our human minds and bodies from the *"deep psychological model of the nine levels of consciousness"* that we have already explored in our previous book.[12]

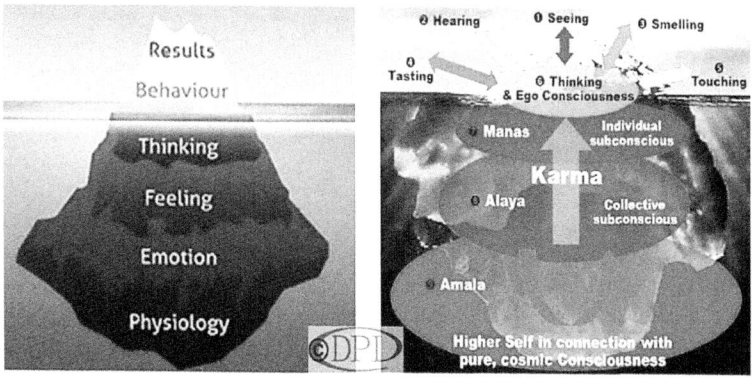

Comparing these two models, you may notice the importance of the Buddhist concept of karma, which is related to the different life-conditions and their tendencies at all cognitive, emotional, and physical levels. This insight makes us realize that if we want to change our karma, whatever form of karma that is, we shouldn't just focus on changing our outlook on life and behavior. Because without changing the associated emotions, all other efforts remain on the surface and cannot contribute to any fundamental improvement in life. And since emotions are deeply related to the heart, we'd better start by changing our heart's electromagnetic field, which not only affects our cognitive and physiological functions, but also attracts our experiences with other people and life situations.

This means that if we want to change what we encounter on the outside, we have to change our own emotions and our states of life. Against this background, it is possible to comprehend why Nichiren points to the need to free oneself from one's own negative states of mind and one's own negative emotions through the Buddhist practice in order to become the "master of your heart".

Chapter 3
Heart coherence and Heart Rate Variability

The believing heart refers to a pure heart

When we dedicate ourselves to the practice of chanting Daimoku, we often do this to cope with everyday challenges and to fulfill our deep desires. To do this, Nichiren always advises us to *"awake and deepen our faith or believing hearts."* But what does that mean in concrete terms? And how can we put that into practice? Let's take Nichiren's further advice on these questions.

> Whether or not your prayer is answered will depend on your *believing heart* [*shinjin*]. I, Nichiren, cannot in any way be held responsible for your failure. When the water is clear, the moon is reflected. […] The heart of all of you are like the water. When your *faith* [*shin*] is weak, it's like muddy water. When your *believing heart* is pure, it is like clear water.
> *Reply to the Lay Nun Nichigon*, WND I, p.1079

Nichiren often uses a natural phenomenon as a metaphor to get his point across, but also to make it easy for everyone to understand. In this example he compares our faith or *believing heart* to the water reflecting the moon clearly or blurred depending on whether the water is pure and clear or polluted and dirty. You may take this metaphor just as an analogy or a symbolic image, but as we will explain in detail later, our heart communicates with the cosmic consciousness that answers our prayer. So far, we cannot complain about Nichiren or anyone else, but must take the challenge on ourselves.

Nichiren continues to say:

> [A sutra says]: "If the hearts of sentient beings are impure, their land is also impure, but when their hearts are pure, so is their land." Thus, although one speaks of the pure and the impure land, there are not two different lands. The difference lies solely in the good or bad of our hearts.
> *On Attaining Buddhahood in This Lifetime*, WDN I: 4

Whether our heart is pure or impure determines not only our personal success and psycho-physiological health, but also how we experience our living conditions in our natural and social environment. This is also a strong message that we actually make decisions about the situation we find ourselves in. Each of us is always faced with the challenge of taking responsibility for life's situation, whatever it may be. And for this purpose, Nichiren provided us with the tool to purify the water reflecting the moon. This principle also applies precisely to the mirror example discussed above: *We can polish our heart's mirror by chanting Nam-myōhō-renge-kyō to manifest the enlightened equality of a Buddha.*.

Thus, Nichiren metaphorically describes the pure heart as crystal clear water and a polished mirror also as the source of the solution to all problems we encounter. This leads us to the following insight:

> Faith or the believing heart refers to a "pure heart" without doubts and illusions. From a cardiological point of view, a *pure heart* with positive emotions corresponds exactly to the state of *heart coherence*.

What is coherence?

As for the term "coherence", we already explained it in the context of brain coherence as "whole brain synchronization"[13] when the two parts of your brain work together in a harmonious way, emitting the same frequency. In general, however, coherence simply means that the different parts of a system work together harmoniously and synchronously. If the individual parts of a system do not work together harmoniously, there will be disturbances and interferences within the system, which lead to energy loss and malfunction of the entire system. Then we speak of "incoherence". Heart coherence therefore means a harmonious, even rhythm of the heart and a well-ordered electromagnetic field of the heart.

You can imagine a rowing team where each team member does whatever they feel like doing. In this case, the boat would not proceed successfully. However, if they work together in sync, they can move the boat efficiently and make it go fast.

Rowing in a team

This spiritual unity of many different individuals is also important for Nichiren and is called "many in body but one in heart" (*Itai-dōshin*) as opposed to "one in body but different in heart" (*Dōtai-ishin*).

> If the different individuals share the same heart, they can all achieve their goals successfully, while the people with different hearts cannot achieve anything despite being in one physical unit. *Many in Body, One in Mind*, WND I, p.618

Nichiren points to examples from the wars of ancient China, in which victory or defeat was not decided by the number of soldiers but by their spiritual unity. This is certainly a universal principle that can be applied to all areas of activity, such as teamwork in business projects and social life, but also to our body to maintain all life-sustaining functions. Thus, the Buddhist term *Itai-dōshin* can be understood as "coherence" in the sense of a harmonious and dynamic interaction of all those involved to achieve the common goal.

When it comes to heart coherence, HeartMath researchers found that our heart rhythms respond in an amazingly accurate way to our thoughts and emotions. Many contemporary scientists believe that Heart Coherence is the underlying state of our physiological processes that determines the quality and stability of the feelings and emotions we experience. The feelings we label as positive actually reflect body states that are coherent, meaning that the regulation of our life processes becomes "efficient, free-flowing and easy," and the feelings we label as "negative," such as anger, anxiety and frustration are examples of incoherent states. But why is the state of coherence so important?

> Coherence basically means that the different parts of a system work together harmoniously and synchronously.

Heart Rate and Heart Rate Variability

HeartMath researchers also found out that you can measure the degree of *Heart Coherence* according to the *Heart Rate Variability* (HRV). It reflects the emotional state of a person and the degree of stress this person is experiencing. The higher the Heart Rate Variability (HRV), the higher the state of coherence. But what exactly is Heart Rate Variability?

The heart rate variability (HRV) measures the gap *between* the heart beats. The gaps between your heart beats vary. If you look at your heart rate over time you will see that your heart rate will vary up and down.

When we have a look at the heart- the heart does not beat like a metronome – not exactly the same beat again and again– in fact our heart beats in a very variable way- this is what we call Heart Rate Variability (HRV).

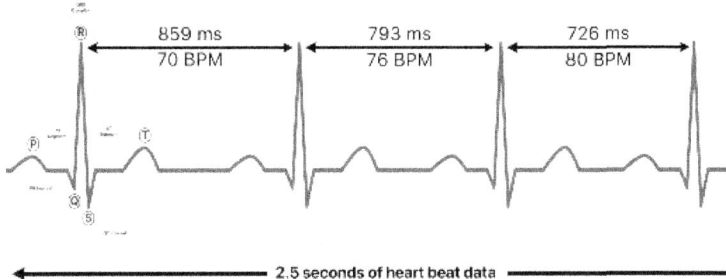

Your heart beat needs to be flexible because HRV is the ability to adapt to a changing environment. Your inner and your outer environment is constantly changing. If you cannot adapt to it, you are in stress. Research about HRV is therefore based on the assumption that a more dynamic system is healthy and a lot of data supports this. The more your heart beat can adopt to a changing environment in a flexible and dynamic way, the healthier your whole body is. This is why exercise and physical movement is also a means to increase your heart rate variability, because it requires adjustment and higher flexibility of your heart beat and therefore increases your heart rate variability.

Therefore, Heart rate variability (HRV) has nothing to do with the number of heart beats, it does not show you how many beats per minute (bpm) your heart beats, but it shows you the way one heart beat changes to the next.

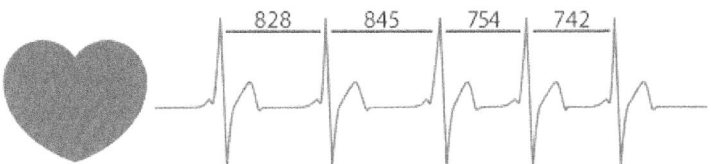

The gaps between your heart beats vary.

There is a variation in the gaps between the heart beats. This time interval between consecutive heart beats is measured in milliseconds. If your heart is accelerating, the gaps between the heart beats will get smaller. If your heart is slowing down, the gaps between your heart beats will get bigger.

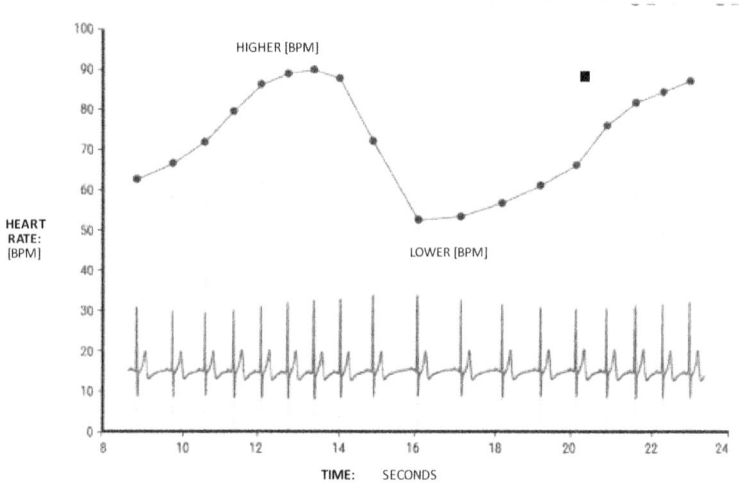

SOURCE: HEART RATE VARIABILITY MCCRATY AND SINGER

To give you an example using the graph[14] above: As you can see in the curve above, when we breathe in, our heartbeat increases and the gaps between the heartbeats become closer to each other. On the contrary, when we breathe out (in the middle), our heartbeat decreases and the distance between the heartbeats become larger. There constantly is an increase and decrease of our heartbeat.

There is interest in HRV in the field of psycho-physiology, because HRV is also related to emotional arousal. HRV provides the continual, bidirectional communication between the heart and the brain, which allows the individual to precisely adapt to changes in their internal environment, which means to their feelings and thoughts, and to changes in their external environment by integrating neural and cardiovascular reactions. This is why HRV is also an indicator of your neuro-cardiological health.

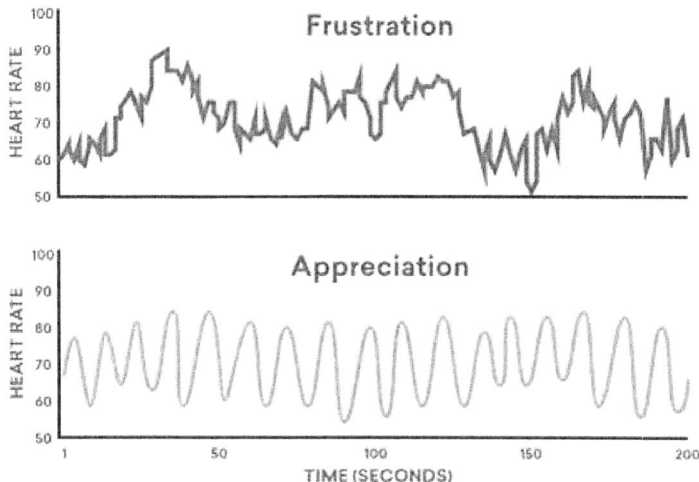

As mentioned before, your heart does not beat in the same rhythm as a metronome but varies according to your emotional reactions. When you are angry or stressed, the heart beats violently and rapidly, while in a relaxed mode, you feel a calm and slow sinus-like heart beat in coherence, as you can see in the graph above.

> The interesting aspect is that the way your heart accelerates or slows down has also something to do with your emotions and stress reactions.

A marker for longevity and biological aging
If you have a look again at the graph above, the curve showing an increase and a decrease of the heartbeat is not the same for

everybody. In fact, if we measure it, it is actually a good indicator of your general health and your mental fitness. It also tells you something about how resilient you are, about your ability to recover and regain your strength and momentum after a physiological or psychological setback.

> Very concretely, it tells us something about our ability to adapt to stress and to external demands– it is a marker for our resilience – and a marker for longevity and biological aging.[15]

The HRV of a person at the age of 70 will naturally not look like that of a 20-year-old. It is a natural progression that HRV decreases by about 5% every year. As we will see later, HRV is also an important measure of our neuro-cardiological health. Most important, however, it is an indicator of how long you have left to live. A 24-hour HRV measurement can actually show a trend of your estimated lifespan.

But the most interesting thing: It can not only be measured, but also trained and positively changed. It is influenced by our breathing patterns and by physical exercise, but also significantly by our thoughts and emotions. This opens the door to how we can positively train the variability of our heartbeat and do something for our own energy management.

The nervous systems of our body

How is it that HRV is connected to our emotions and stress responses? In what way are our emotions related to the gaps between our heart beats? Well, the extent to which our heart accelerates and slows down is also controlled by our emotions. Therefore, HRV is ultimately an indicator of the balance of our autonomic nervous system[16]. You may be wondering: what exactly is the autonomous nervous system (ANS) and what are its functions?

The Sympathetic and the Parasympathetic Nervous System

The Autonomic Nervous System (ANS) is a control system that acts largely unconsciously and regulates bodily functions such as heart rate, digestion, respiration, the immune system, endocrine system, blood pressure, etc. You don't have to consciously think about these functions for them to work. They just happen automatically. The Autonomic Nervous System regulates 90% of the body´s internal processes. It signals the body to speed up or slow down, depending on the situation. Emotions change its activity and more than 1400 biochemical changes are set in motion by our changing emotions.

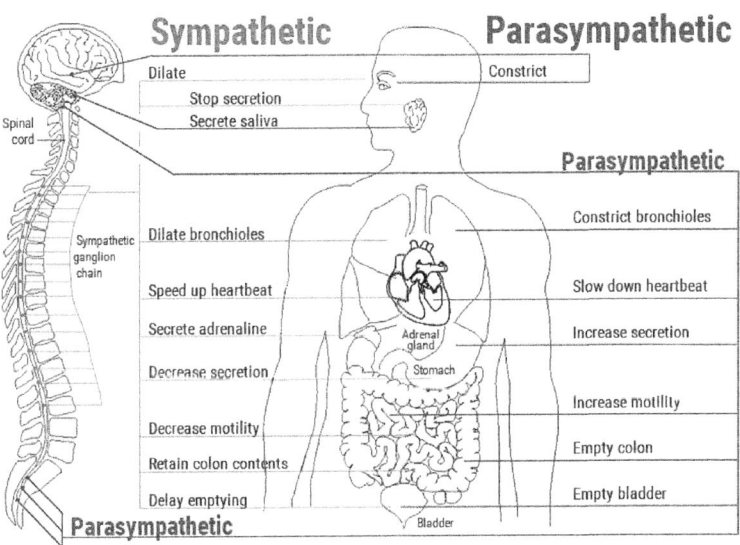

The ANS is subdivided into the *sympathetic nervous system* (SNS) for mobilizing energy in cases of emergencies and the *parasympathetic nervous system* (PNS) is activated when organisms are in a relaxed state.

When you see a real danger or something you perceive as threatening, the amygdala in your brain tells the autonomic nervous system to activate the sympathetic nervous system. And what will that do? It prepares your body for either fighting, flight, or freezing. So, what will happen? You begin to breathe faster, your heart rate increases, your blood pressure changes, adrenalin rushes, your digestion slows down, you are ready to fight, to flee the situation or to just freeze and be paralyzed. The astonishing thing is that these reactions can be turned on just by thought alone.

> The sympathetic nervous system is aroused
> by fear, anger, hostility and pain.

When you chronically live in a fight or flight mode, you turn down the capacity for your body's cells to do their job of taking in nutrition and to release toxins.

However, if you manage to get yourself into a safe state, the parasympathetic nervous system (PNS) kicks in. And what does the parasympathetic do? It does the exact opposite of what the sympathetic nervous system does: Your heart rate will slow down again, your digestion will reactivate, your blood pressure will drop, you will stop sweating, you will breathe normally again, not so fast anymore.

We need both functions well-coordinated!

The Sympathetic Nervous System can be seen as the gas pedal, because it is responsible for activity but also for stress. The Parasympathetic Nervous System is responsible for regeneration, but also for providing energy, as it also controls digestion. When it is activated, you are in the "rest and digest mode".

Since these two branches are antagonists, rarely both are active at the same time, rather there is a tendency for one or the other to dominate and in today's world of hectic, pressure, anxiety and stress, the sympathetic nervous system tends to dominate.

> We notice a strong dominance of the Sympathetic Nervous System when we can no longer relax, when we no longer sleep well at night or when we feel constantly nervous.

It is important to bring our Autonomic Nervous System into balance again. You need the Sympathetic Nervous System when you are active and you also need moments of balance, the Parasympathetic Nervous System. It's not about constantly relaxing, but about reducing too much tension.

If we did not have the Sympathetic Nervous System, then our body would not prepare us to fight, flight or freeze. And without the Parasympathetic Nervous System we would not know how to relax and regenerate.

However, today we have so many factors that keep our Sympathetic Nervous System active *all the time*. When you feel frustrated, worried, angry, whenever you feel under stress, you experience an effect of the Sympathetic Nervous System being too active. For stress arises not only in direct response to external situations or events, but also due to internal ongoing habitual emotional processes and attitudes. Recurring feelings of worry, and anxiety; anger, judging others all the time, and feelings of resentment; discontent and unhappiness; insecurity and self-doubt often consume a large part of our emotional energy. Constantly worrying about your job or your future and constantly thinking about the problems you have with your spouse, your children or your boss, puts your Autonomic Nervous System out of balance.

HRV is an indicator of your ANS balance

Since your Heart Rate Variability (HRV) is strongly connected to your emotions, it is also an indicator of the balance between the sympathetic and the parasympathetic nervous system. When you are under stress and your sympathetic activity increases, your HRV decreases. The same happens the other way around. When you incorporate relaxation in your life and manage your emotions well and the activity of your parasympathetic activity increases, then your HRV increases. When there is too much activity of the Sympathetic Nervous System, then your autonomic nervous system is out of balance.

The global health crisis of chronic diseases

Human wellbeing today is endangered due to a huge increase in what are so-called chronic diseases which include cardiovascular diseases, cancer, type II diabetes and dementia, mostly in the form of Alzheimer´s disease. If you think about the fact that chronic diseases contribute to 74% of all deaths worldwide and in some countries to even more than 90% of deaths, then you may realize that we are in a real global health crisis (WHO, 2022).

The figures are really alarming. According to the German Robert Koch Institute, every second German man or woman is predicted to get cancer in his or her life.

According to a forecast by the World Health Organization (WHO), the number of cancer cases worldwide is expected to almost double by 2040.[17] This is the result of the World Cancer Report of the International Agency for Research on Cancer (IARC), which is compiled every five years. In 2018, 18.1 million people worldwide were newly diagnosed with cancer, 9.6 million people died of it. In 2040, about 29 to 37 million people are likely to be newly diagnosed with cancer, reports the IARC on World Cancer Day on 4 February.

In the coming years, more and more people will also develop dementia. This is the result of a study by the World Health Organization (WHO). By 2030, around 40 percent more people worldwide are likely to be living with dementia than today – that's in about nine years. In 2019, around 55 million people worldwide were affected.

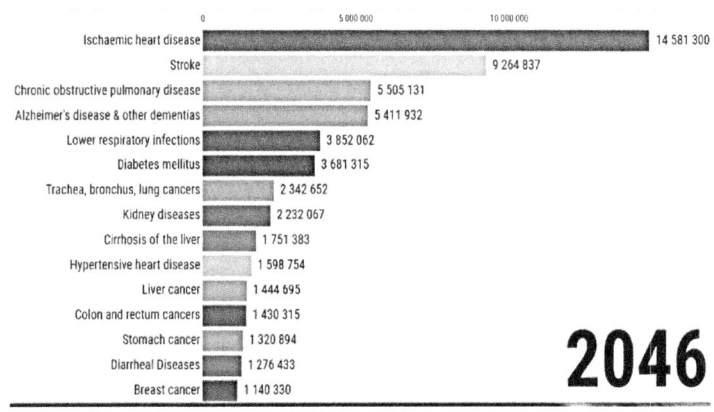

Top 15 deadliest diseases in the future

However, cardiovascular diseases are the leading cause of death worldwide, accounting for 32% of all global deaths. 85% of these deaths were due to heart attacks and strokes.

CARDIOVASCULAR DISEASE
THE WORLD'S NUMBER 1 KILLER

Cardiovascular diseases are a group of disorders of the heart and blood vessels, commonly referred to as **heart disease** and **stroke**.

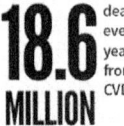
18.6 MILLION deaths every year from CVD

33% of all global deaths

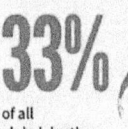
>75% of CVD deaths take place in low- and middle-income countries

GLOBAL CAUSES OF DEATH

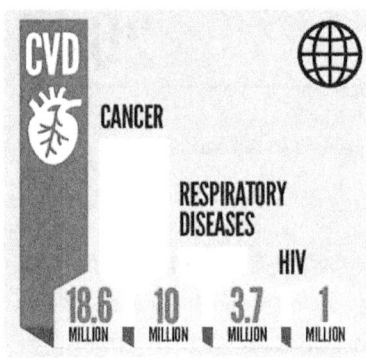

CVD — 18.6 MILLION
CANCER — 10 MILLION
RESPIRATORY DISEASES — 3.7 MILLION
HIV — 1 MILLION

RISK FACTORS FOR CVD

 High Blood Pressure
 Unhealthy Diet
 High Cholesterol
 Diabetes
 Overweight & Obesity
 Tobacco
 Air Pollution
 Kidney Disease
 Physical Inactivity
 Harmful use of alcohol

Sources: World Health Organization; IHME, Global Burden of Disease

info@worldheart.org
www.worldheart.org

f worldheartfederation
🐦 worldheartfed
📷 worldheartfederation

The limits of conventional medicine

Conventional medicine is primarily concerned with the physical symptoms from a mechanistic and biochemical view. Therefore, the diagnosed diseases can only be treated with surgery to remove or completely replace the defective part, or with drugs, most of which have negative side effects that damage the liver, kidneys, stomach and intestines.

These medical treatments may be necessary for diagnosed diseases, but today, depending on the physical condition, we can take many preventive measures such as physical exercise, taking supplementary vitamins and minerals, healthy foods without sugar and artificial substances and getting rid of toxins in our bodies, let alone stopping drinking alcohol and smoking. With these changes alone, many diseases could be prevented or improved, though we also seem to live in a lifestyle crisis where making these changes is just so difficult for many.

But just changing your lifestyle and diet can make a huge contribution to your health and will also lead to an increase in HRV which, as mentioned earlier, is an overall biomarker of your health and fitness. There is a study showing that various aspects of diet have been shown to improve HRV both acutely and over the longer term, such as losing weight and switching to a Mediterranean diet, as well as including Omega-3 fatty acids, B-vitamins and probiotics in your daily regimen.[18]

However, even a lot of people who do their best on a physical and biochemical level become seriously ill. How come? I will always remember one of my neighbors who was known for doing everything she could to look after her health on a physical level. She was almost obsessed with eating only organic foods and exercising regularly. However, she became seriously ill with stomach cancer and died at the age of 43. I knew she had many unresolved emotional issues and wondered what led to her illness.

I began think about the internal, emotional, mental and, in our case, psycho-energetic conditions for illness and healing. A more holistic view on health would also take emotional aspects into account, because as already mentioned:

Our mind is not separated from our body.

The effects of an ANS imbalance

Illness is often strongly linked to our emotions. An imbalance in your ANS tends to result in disease. Therefore, it is often our uncontrolled emotions that trigger stress and illness. As we have already learned, a low HRV is an indicator of an imbalance in your ANS. There is growing evidence that a number of diseases are accompanied with HRV declines, including diabetes, cardiovascular disease and psychiatric disorders, amongst others.[19]

The number one cause of death in Western society is cardiovascular diseases, which in turn are accompanied by a decrease in HRV.[20]

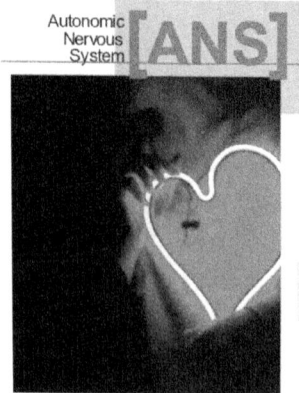

Autonomic Nervous System [ANS] **dysfunction** is associated with...
ALZHEIMER'S / CANCER
DEPRESSION / DIABETES
HEART DISEASE / STROKE

Lower HRV is also associated with inflammation, which is linked with the progression of atherosclerosis, rheumatoid arthritis, and cancer.[21]

Our Parasympathetic Nervous System reacts sensitively to harmful influences. Chronic stress, lack of exercise, an unfavorable lifestyle and various diseases lead to "parasympathetic dysfunction". If this malfunction of the Parasympathetic Nervous System lasts longer, your health suffers. There is now substantiated evidence that an overactivity of the Parasympathetic Nervous System and reduced parasympathetic activity leads to an imbalance in the Autonomic Nervous System, which is also causally linked to the occurrence of cancer, stroke, multiple sclerosis, depression and Alzheimer's disease.[22]

In case of cancer, overactivity of both the sympathetic and the parasympathetic nervous system, both of which can lead to an imbalance of the Autonomic Nervous System, is linked to the initiation and growth of cancer cells.[23]

> The key to health is therefore a balance of the Autonomic Nervous System.

In addition, an imbalance between your Sympathetic Nervous System and your Parasympathetic Nervous System is also linked to sleep disorders, panic attacks, fatigue, irritable bowel syndrome, migraines, and cardiac arrythmia.[24] HRV is therefore considered to be an effective biomarker of general stress and health.[25]

> A low HRV indicates that there is an imbalance in your Autonomic Nervous System.[26]

HOW STRESS AFFECTS THE BODY

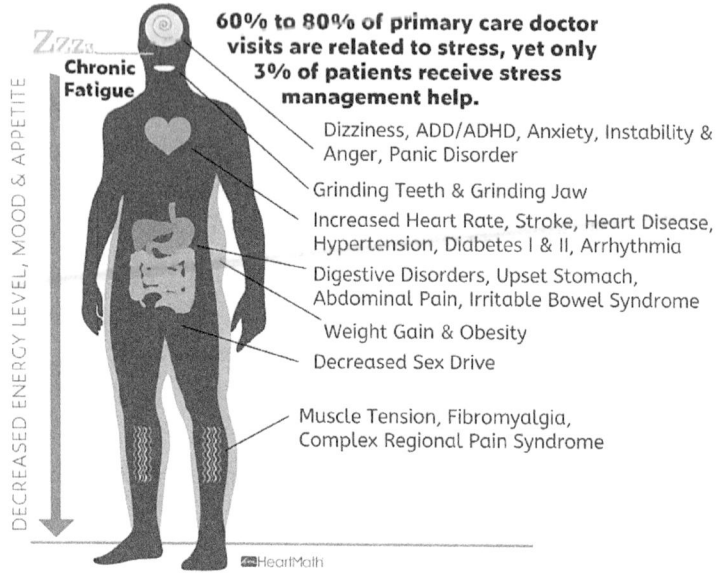

Comparing an exhausted and an energetic person

To illustrate such an imbalance, you can see below the measurement of the Sympathetic Nervous System and the Parasympathetic Nervous System of an unhealthy, exhausted person. This measurement was translated into a graphic image of "life fire"[27] that vividly depicts decreased sympathetic (red bar) and parasympathetic (green bar) activity.

In this case, you can clearly see that in an unhealthy, exhausted person, the activity in both the sympathetic (red bar) and parasympathetic (green bar) nervous system is very low. In the green bar there is hardly any parasympathetic activity, not even during hours of sleep, which is a strong indication that this person has little opportunity for regeneration and recovery. This

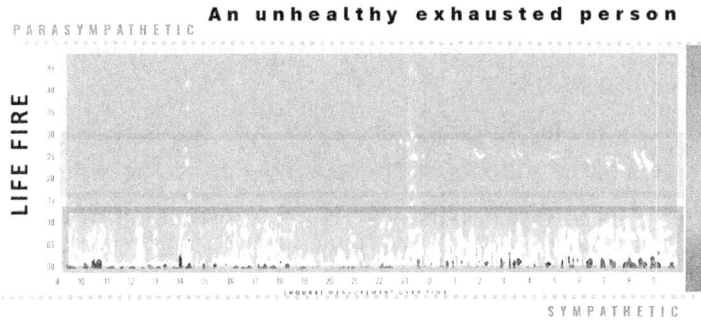

Both branches of the ANS are extremely low, leaving the person barely able to be active or to recover.

person has hardly any reserves and resources. However, sympathetic activity is also reduced. As you can see, overall sympathetic activity is relatively low and reduced, although sympathetic activity can dominate since there is little parasympathetic activity left. This person simply lacks energy and vitality during the day. And even at night during sleep there is no regeneration and storage of energy, since parasympathetic activity is not really activated even during sleep. This person has very limited reserves available right now. This looks like "burnout" that will definitely lead to illness if he or she doesn't find a way to build up some resources and energy again.

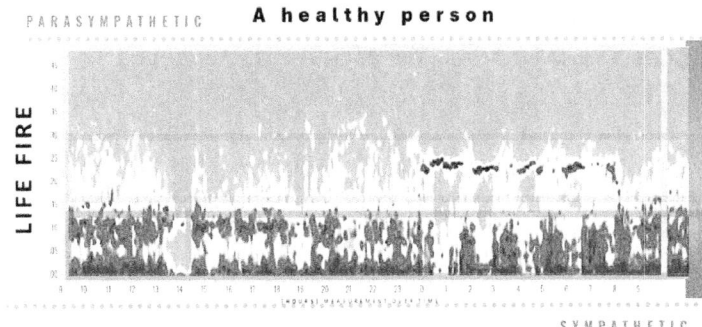

Both branches of the ANS are extremely low, leaving the person barely able to be active or to recover.

In contrast to the example above, you see the HRV measurement of a healthy, energetic person who has a lot of energy and resources available.

In this case in the graph above you can see here that both branches of the Autonomic Nervous System are activated and provide energy and regeneration at the same time. The Sympathetic Nervous System (red bar) is highly activated. This person has a lot of energy during the day. The Parasympathetic Nervous System is also activated, especially during the sleep hours (green bar). This means that regeneration and relaxation take place at night and that this person has many reserves and resources at their disposal to cope with everyday stress.

The question now is: How can you build up reserves and resources again when you are under complete stress? Since Heart Rate Variability (HRV) is an indicator of your physical, but also your mental and emotional health, what can you do to positively influence and increase it? For the variability of your heart can be changed by physical exercise, but it is also very sensitive to your emotions, even responding to changes in the rhythm of your breathing.

Well, even a simple exercise like breathing in a harmonious and coherent rhythm, inhaling for about 5 seconds and exhaling for 5 seconds can have a tremendous positive impact on your heart's variability and flexibility, instantly increasing your resources. We will do that later together and examine it.

Chapter 4
HRV analysis of Daimoku

Comparison of HRV changes in four cases

Since Heart Rate Variability (HRV) is a general indicator of our mental and physical health, including our life expectancy, we thought it would be interesting to establish whether there were any changes after chanting Daimoku.

To find out, we compared four different cases.[28] First, we measured HRV during normal activity, such as working at a computer. Then we did a coherent breathing exercise for ten minutes, inhaling and exhaling for five seconds each. Afterwards, we chanted Daimoku alone for ten minutes. And finally, we chanted together to see how it would affect the respective HRV values.

HRV analysis offers many different measures, but we only chose those parameters that were most important for our comparison and listed them in the table below.

	Measurement 1: Regular Activity	Measurement 2: Relaxed Breathing	Measurement 3: Chanting Alone	Measurement 4: Group Chanting
SDNN [ms] Average heart rate variation [HRV]	33.2	54.8	59.3	69.4
pNN50 [%] PNS vs. SNS = more resilient state	9.72	17.29	39.44	48.04
RMSSD [ms] Time difference between heartbeats	48.1	43.8	67.8	80.8
Stress Index More stressed state	10.0	8.4	7.5	7.0
Total Power [ms^2]	592	2826	2409	3331

We will briefly explain their meaning and compare the respective values achieved in each case.

HRV parameters

HRV analysis is based on the heart rate data (bpm) only and the most widely used methods for HRV analysis can be grouped under *time-domain* and *frequency-domain*.

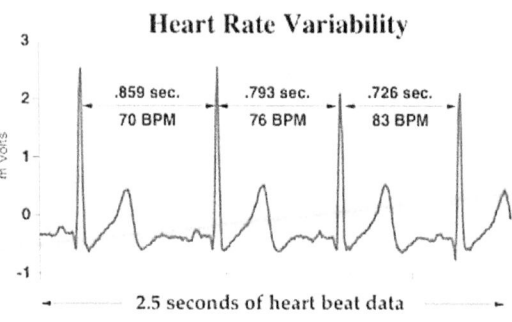

HRV is measured in different ways utilising different parameters. In our investigations, we focused on *time-domain* and *frequency-domain* measurements in identifying whether chanting contributed to elevations in HRV.

SDNN

The SDNN value belongs to the time-domain related standards in HRV measurement. Often calculated over a 24-hour period, SDNN reflects all the cyclic components responsible for variability in the period of recording; therefore, it represents total variability of your heartbeat.

> The SDNN value provides information about the overall variability of the heartbeat. It shows how well the autonomic nervous system can regulate processes in the body.

The more the SDNN increases, the greater the variability. This also means that the adaptability and flexibility of the autonomic nervous system increases. The greater the variability, the more easily and flexibly it can adapt to incoming stressors and changes in the environment. The more the SDNN decreases, however, the lesser the variability. The SDNN is the "gold standard" for medical stratification of cardiac risk when recorded over a 24-hour period. SDNN values predict both morbidity and mortality. Based on 24 hour monitoring, patients with SDNN values below 50 ms (milliseconds) are classified as unhealthy, 50–100 ms have compromised health, and above 100 ms, are healthy.

What is a good [SDNN] value?

BASED ON 24 HOUR MONITORING, PATIENTS WITH [SDNN] VALUES:

ABOVE 100 MS ARE HEALTHY
50–100 MS HAVE COMPROMISED HEALTH
BELOW 50 MS ARE CLASSIFIED AS UNHEALTHY

The SDNN value shows how well the sympathetic and the parasympathetic nervous system work together. The higher the SDNN, the better they work together. In cardiology, it is an important value for assessing your chances of survival after a heart attack.

Now let´s have a look at our data. On the day that we carried out our analysis, I was aware that working at the computer all day and concentrating on the task at hand, had somehow drained my energy reserves. We registered the SDNN value at 33.2 ms, indicating a lower life-condition. After breathing in the above-mentioned rhythm for ten minutes, my SDNN level rose to 54.8 ms. There was an even greater increase when I spent the same time, chanting alone: to 59.3 ms. However, when we chanted together, the rise was even greater: to 69.4 ms. This result shows the effectiveness of the practice of chanting Daimoku and evidences the fact that chanting together is even more effective. This demonstrates that when you continue with the dynamic and harmonious rhythm of Daimoku, you will raise your energy.

> Overall, the SDNN value increased by 200% when we chanted Daimoku together for only 10 minutes.

pNN50

The pNN50 also belongs to the time-related standards. It shows the general power reserves of your body. Higher values indicate increased parasympathetic activity. In general, your pNN50 should be above 20%.

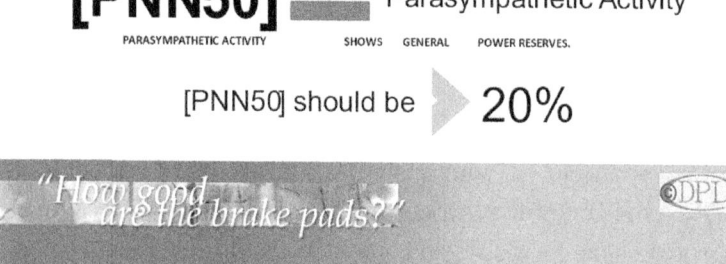

This is how asking: How good is your breaking power and how good are the brake pads on your brakes? In this case, the pNN50 would describe the quality of the brakes. Are your brake pads still thick and firm or are they already worn out? If your pNN50 value is low, you are either tired or over-stressed. In general, you may say: The pNN50 is very sustainable. First signs of deterioration can be quickly seen in a decrease of this value. Whenever you get exhausted and use up your power reserves, you can see it in your pNN50 measure.

It is remarkable how your pNN50 values drop as part of the natural aging process: by 74.6 % in men and by 72.6% in women between the ages of 20 and 64.[29] In this context, it is important to understand that a decline in parasympathetic activity can be counteracted by coherent breathing alone, but even more effectively by the Nichiren Buddhist practice of chanting Daimoku.

First, we measured the coherent breathing method. Ten minutes of coherent breathing exercise resulted in an increase in the body´s general reserves: the value increased from 9.72% to 17.9 %. However, after chanting alone and together for 10 minutes, this value increased even further. After chanting alone for 10 minutes, the pNN50 rose to 39.44 % and after chanting together for ten minutes, it rose to 48.04%. This means:

> During the process of chanting Daimoku together for 10 minutes, the power reserves in my body had increased by 394%.

RMSSD

Next, we looked at the RMSSD value after doing the coherent breathing exercise for 10 minutes. The RMSSD value is a standard measure for parasympathetic heart regulation and an indicator for recovery and regeneration. The RMSSD value shows how quickly the body can react to stress. A high value means that the body can cope well with the alternation of stress and relief. It therefore tells you something about how stressed you are. It is reduced when you are physically and emotionally exhausted.

[RMSSD] Indicator for Recovery, Fitness, Health and Regeneration

Let's stay with the comparison with the brakes in the car: the pNN50 value stands for the quality of the brakes or your inner power reserves while RMSSD value stands for the breaking force.

If you have a good RMSSD value like 40 ms, the body can handle the alternation of stress and relief. This means that even when you experience a stressful situation, you can recover quickly from it and soon bounce back. Very low RMSSD values, however, such as 8 ms, indicate that the body is no longer able to recover sufficiently. This also applies to your emotional reactivity and to how well you can recover from emotional stress. How long are you staying depressed when you have had an argument with your best friend or your partner? How much does the stress with your coworker or boss affect you? RMSSD is also considered to represent the function of the vagus nerve; the so-called vagal tone, which may offer insight into your physical, neurological and emotional health.

Because the vagus nerve is so important to the gut-brain connection and other connections in the body, there may be a higher risk of conditions such as gastrointestinal disfunction, heart disease, depression, and anxiety, when the vagus nerve isn't working properly, Therefore, low RMSSD has also been strongly associated with major depression.[30]

Now, looking at our comparative data, surprisingly, my RMSSD value dropped after the breathing exercise from 48.1 ms to 43.8 ms. This was the first time that the breathing exercise had no elevating effect on my HRV reading. In contrast, when I chanted alone, the RMSSD value increased from 48.1 ms to 67.8 ms. However, when we chanted together, the RMSSD value increased even further - to 80.8 ms.

> The RMSSD value increased by 168% after chanting Daimoku together for 10 minutes. This means I had a 168% increase in my ability to recover from stress and to bounce back after 10 minutes of Daimoku.

Stress index

The stress index (SI) is a measure of the tension in the regulatory systems of the human organism. It is related to the regulatory activity of the sympathetic nervous system (SNS) in response to physical or mental stress. The higher the stress index, the higher the activity of the regulatory channels connected to the sympathetic nervous system. The lower the stress index (SI), the higher the activity of the regulatory channels related to the parasympathetic nervous system (PNS) and hormones. Even small loads of physical or emotional stress, can double the stress index.

In our data my baseline stress index was 10.0 and this dropped to 8.4 after breathing in a coherent rhythm with a meditative mind. However, when chanting alone, the stress index dropped to 7.5 and even further to 7.0 when chanting together. This means that I was able to lower my own stress index by 3 points from 10.0 to 7.0. Chanting for 10 minutes helped me transform the tense and exhausted feeling I was left with after working on the computer all day.

Chanting Daimoku represents a useful and efficient means to reduce the effects and symptoms of stress, to fight depression and to help you recover both physically and emotionally.

Total Power

Finally, we also looked at the change in a value known as "total power". This is a frequency-domain related method of assessing HRV and reflects the overall variability of the heart rate pattern over the length of the recording.

The "total power" is a general guideline for the ability of the autonomic nervous system to regulate processes in the body and it indicates the adaptability of the autonomic nervous system in a changing environment.

When you are exhausted, not getting enough sleep or after a hearty meal, for instance, your "total energy" naturally decreases. According to a study by S.B. Park et al., healthy people in South Korea with an average age of 45 years (one of the most stressed societies worldwide) have an average total power of only 1100 ms^2. On the contrary, for a balanced, athletic and healthy adult in a recovered state, the readings are often over 3000 ms^2 within a five-minute measurement.

Total Power

- Shows how well the autonomic nervous system can regulate processes in the body
- Indicates the adaptability of the autonomic nervous system.
- Increased by 560% after 10 minutes of Daimoku

When we measured the change in total power during the coherent breathing exercise, we found it increased from 592 ms^2 to 2826 ms^2; an amazing improvement of 477%. There was no increase when chanting alone, but a dramatic increase to 3331 ms^2 when chanting together for 10 minutes. This was an improvement of 560% compared to the original baseline when working on the computer.

You will grow younger

If you consider that HRV is an indicator of your life span and of your cardiovascular health and that HRV decreases by 5% every year, it is astonishing that Total Power, which means the adaptability of your Autonomic Nervous System, can be increased by more than 500% (five times) by chanting Daimoku for 10 minutes. In our experiment, the SDNN value, representing the activity of the sympathetic nervous system (SNS), increased by 200% and the RMSSD, representing the parasympathetic activity (indicating recovery and regeneration), increased by 160%.

There is a proven connection between the heart rhythm and the mental, emotional and physiological processes in the body. The gap between your heartbeats, the heart rate variability which also indicates the rhythm of your heart, reacts in a very sensitive way to your changing emotional state. Many scientists and medical experts use an analysis of your HRV as an important measuring instrument for detecting mental, emotional and physical stress.

Therefore, the HRV has become an exact indicator of the state of your Autonomic Nervous System and has even become an instrument for predicting how long you are going to live. This means, the higher your HRV, the longer you are expected to live. Indeed, a higher HRV has been found to be associated with reduced mortality, improved psychological well-being and a higher quality of life.

Up until we carried out these measurements, I had not associated my likely life span directly with the emotions I experienced every day. However, there is an intimate connection between the two that made me truly understand Nichiren's request that we become masters of our hearts and learn to regulate our emotions.

Our measurements showed me that Nichiren was actually right when he said that by chanting Daimoku you will become rejuvenated and accumulate good fortune.

Shijō Kingo's wife sent a donation to Nichiren and asked for prayers to protect her from the hardships that might befall her at her difficult age of 33. Although this was a traditional superstition, Nichiren assured her that she had the capacity to turn unfortunate events into lucky ones. He encouraged her by predicting:

> You will grow younger and accumulate good fortune.
> *The Unity of Husband and Wife*
> *(Reply to the wife of Shijō Kingo)*, WND I, p.464

Chapter 5
The power of Heart Coherence

> If the brain is the radio's receiver, then the heart is
> the dial tuning the radio to the frequency of your choice.
> – Nassim Haramein

The heart is your emotional center

Over the past decade, researchers have discovered that the heart plays the primary role in the emotional system. How you feel and what you feel depends to a large extent on the activity of your heart. As mentioned in chapter 2 above, your heart is an information processing center and there are more nerves going from the heart to the brain than vice versa. Your heart is actually your emotional center, shaping your emotions and influencing your brain: it transmits information to your brain and the rest of your body in four different ways: *neurologically* (via the nervous system), *biochemically* (via hormones and neurotransmitters), *biophysically* (via blood pressure), and *energetically* (via electromagnetic fields).

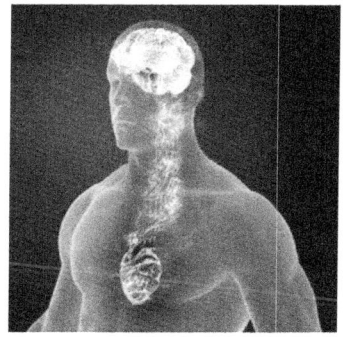

The heart communicates with the brain neurologically, biochemically, biophysical and energetically.

Coherent or incoherent heart rhythm

Do you remember the graph from chapter 3 that shows the Heart Rate Variability (HRV) curve where the intervals between heartbeats become shorter as we breathe in and longer as we breathe out. Have a look at it again:

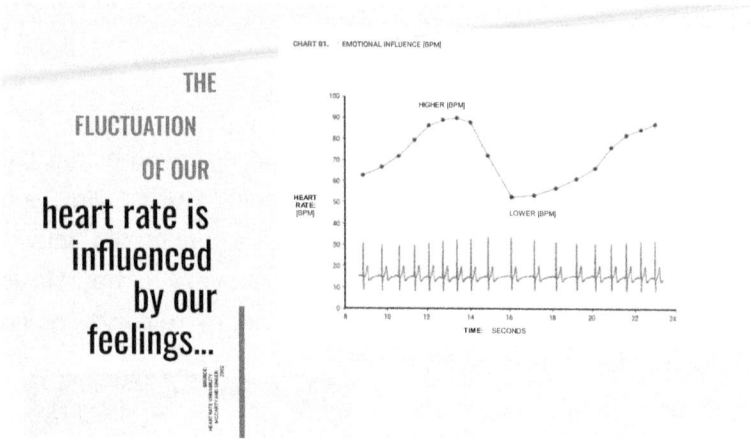

The form and rhythm of this curve is strongly dependent on our emotions. Research has shown that stress and different kinds of emotion are reflected in our heart rhythm pattern. This is because what we are feeling, causes changes in the activity in our nervous system, which affects the heart rhythm pattern.

This pattern is transmitted from the heart to the higher brain centers and influences the way the brain processes information. Feelings of frustration and anxiety cause the heart rhythm to be incoherent and to become more disordered, jagged, and irregular, thus inhibiting the higher brain center's ability to function properly. This is called an incoherent heart rhythm pattern.

Moreover, this causes a drain in our energy levels. This is how our heart rhythm pattern looks (on the left-hand side) when we are frustrated, angry or anxious. On the right-hand side, is how the heart rhythm pattern looks when we are filled with a feeling of appreciation, love and care. There is a huge difference which shows itself in our heart rhythm pattern.

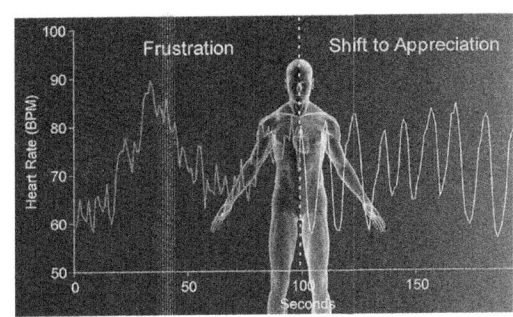

Heart coherence is a state of harmonious alignment between your heart, your mind, your emotions and your entire body.

It is the underlying state of our physiological processes that determines the quality and stability of the feelings and emotions we experience. It essentially determines the quality of our lives.

Your brain responds to the rhythm of your heart

You heart rhythm has a tremendous effect on your brain. This is because your brain monitors and interprets the heart rhythm pattern. It compares a pattern transmitted to it by the heart with the patterns it has already stored, and often elicits an emotion based on the pattern's match. This means, if you tend to get annoyed often, then that's the feeling triggered by an incoherent rhythm pattern in your heart. If you tend to feel sad and anxious, your brain will quickly recognize that feeling and trigger it in response to an incoherent heartbeat.

Your emotions determine your energy

I have often experienced this. When someone or something annoys me, when I am fearful or disappointed, when I have an argument with somebody or any other emotional upheaval, this leaves me feeling exhausted and worn out. I feel that all my energy has dissipated.

From an energy-management perspective, depleting emotions are costly and inefficient. Just like a bucket with a lot of holes in it, our energy is pouring out like water through the holes of a bucket.

The more intense our feelings of anger, frustration or anxiety, the greater the drain on our energy. Nonetheless, getting upset on a regular basis tends to wear us out and waste more energy than one, big, emotional outburst.

Positive emotions lead to a coherent heart rhythm

On the other hand, feelings of love and appreciation generate a smooth heart rhythm pattern, which promotes higher brain center functioning, boosting our energy, our capacity to solve problems and our memory. This is called *a coherent heart rhythm pattern*. Positive emotions produce more ordered and coherent, sinus-like heart rhythms, which reduce nervous system chaos and improve our heart function.[31]

These are emotions we all enjoy. They are not just pleasant, but according to latest research, they also increase our energy level and are regenerative down to the cellular level. Those are emotions like love, appreciation, joy, optimism, compassion, forgiveness and gratitude. They are all part of the higher states of life. These heart-centered emotions improve the balance of our nervous system. I always enjoy it when I have been chanting for a couple of minutes and this feeling of joy and optimism rises up from the depth of my being, *independent of external conditions.*

Putting in high positive emotions that put you out of ego:

- ✓ Happiness
- ✓ Appreciation
- ✓ Gratitude
- ✓ Love
- ✓ Inspiration
- ✓ Joy
- ✓ Enthusiasm
- ✓ Certainty

After I first started chanting, I began to relate my state of energy to my emotions. I never realized that my heart was responsible for the energy levels I experienced. Research shows, however, that energy is created automatically through the physiological processes that are occurring in our body continuously. Human beings have the capacity to create a huge amount of energy and according to the HeartMath Institute, the vast majority is created by the heart.

Just like we take in food and oxygen and convert them to energy, we can take in positive emotions and transform them into life energy and joy.

Positive emotions raise our energy levels and increase our energy reserves. We feel vital, flexible, creative and powerful.

Exercise 3

Consider all the situations, events and activities you experienced yesterday and how you felt in each situation.

Make a list of your moods and emotions during each activity.

Did you experience more negative or more positive emotions?

How was your energy level at the end of the day?

Did you experience a change in your mood and in your energy level after chanting Daimoku?

Coherence has an uplifting effect on others

In a coherent state, our life becomes efficient, free-flowing and easy. This feels good for us. But why is it important to feel good - not only for ourselves but also for others? What difference does it make? It´s very easy: Our feelings and emotions are communicated through the electromagnetic field of our heart to our environment. Thus, if we become coherent, this has an uplifting effect on others: establishing personal coherence contributes to social coherence and ultimately, global coherence. The HeartMath Institute confirms that the quality of our thoughts, feelings, attitudes and treatment of others, defines our personal vibrations.

And it is exactly through our personal vibrations that we affect each other and the environment around us. The ways we think, feel and act also define our state of life in Nichiren Buddhism. That´s why we can relate our state of life to our personal vibration.

How you think, feel and act defines your personal vibration

How you think, feel and act defines your personal vibration.

We mentioned in the last chapter that our hearts produce an electromagnetic field. According to the HeartMath Institute, the vibrational pattern of that field changes based on your thoughts, attitudes, emotions and intentions and can affect the mental and emotional states of others around us. You can think of your heart´s magnetic field as your personal field environment. In an experiment, HeartMath found that when three people created a coherent field environment by feeling positive emotions and becoming coherent in their hearts, this had a huge uplifting effect on a fourth person in this environment who was not trained in becoming coherent (the blue figure at the bottom in the picture above). The untrained participant had been feeling unwell and was initially incoherent.

This indicates that your own state of life does not just affect how *you* feel and think; when you send out incoherent feelings, and thoughts full of anger or frustration, or if you do not do what you say (and therefore act incoherently), the people around you will also be negatively affected by your incoherence.

Conversely, once you become coherent; radiating positive feelings and thoughts (such as appreciation, joy, love and care) and acting in a coherent manner, then the people around you will be uplifted without you even saying a word.

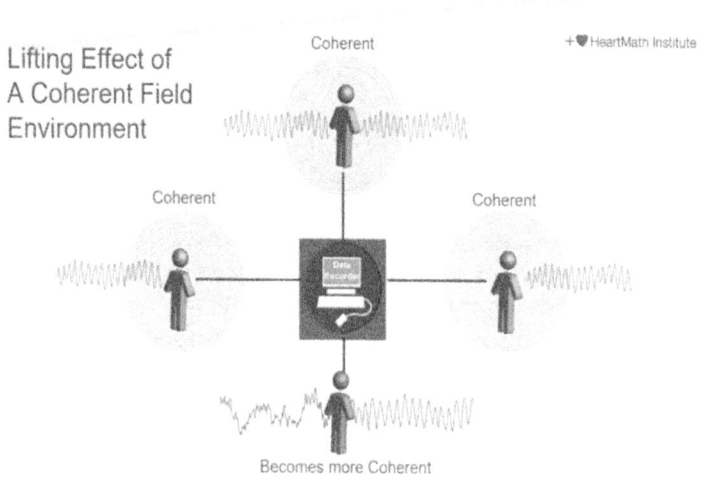

Coherence is the underlying physical condition of the flow state

There are times in our lives when we have experienced periods of being in sync, flowing with a sense of ease through whatever challenges come our way. When we are in that coherent flow, things that come up just don't seem to get under our skin. We are firing on all cylinders. That is what coherence is all about: The heart, mind, emotions and body are all working in sync. When this happens, we are able to "take charge" of ourselves and maintain our composure. We have more energy. Time seems to pass by quickly and we seem to flow through or around challenging issues. When difficulties come up, we can think more clearly, keep our cool, do what we need to do and move on.

> Heart Coherence is a state of harmonious alignment between your heart, your mind, your emotions and your whole body.

Emotions that drain our energy

There are emotions and thoughts that strengthen us and there are others that drain our energy. Negative emotions are those energies that cause physiological stress, such as: anger, frustration, hostility, feelings of guilt, dissatisfaction, resentment, judgment, feeling overwhelmed, apathy, hopelessness, feelings of unworthiness, feeling depressed, jealousy, fear, worry or anxiety - to name just a few! These are all feelings of the lower states of life. Negative feelings take the biggest part of your energy. HeartMath Institute discovered that these negative emotions cause an incoherent heart rhythm and an imbalance in your nervous system. This can lead to serious health problems because when your energy reserves are constantly used up to cope with stress, there is little energy remaining for immune defense and regenerative processes in the body.

When I started chanting, I experienced a profound realization that something was happening inside of me. For the first time in my life, I became acutely *aware* of my emotions. I even registered my fear and my anger. It was a great relief to feel that I succeeded in transforming these negative feelings by chanting Daimoku. Through chanting, I could release old, stored emotions. The feeling of anger, for example, is a pathway that can trap you in old patterns. It is therefore crucial to clear such feelings as soon as you become aware of them. For me, there is nothing that can clear my emotions more efficiently than chanting Daimoku.

Nowadays, I am more conscious of feelings of irritation, frustration or impatience, when they arise. I have noticed that this is when my goals do not tend to manifest as quickly. Beforehand, I was often oblivious of these feelings and as to their influence on the manifestation of my goals. Since I began chanting, I have deepened my awareness of my entrenched thought patterns: By way of example, I often thought that life or someone "had done me wrong" or that I had been "at a disadvantage". In other words, I often felt a "victim". I also became acutely aware that I often worried too much about other people. I realized that I had to change these patterns of thought and feeling by fostering my appreciation and gratitude for the positive things, people and circumstances in my life. However, it is only when the presence of pure consciousness arises while chanting, that I am most successful in engendering such positive feelings. Whenever I blame other people or circumstances for a negative situation that arises in my life, anger or pain start to build up in me. Even though my feelings of anger are often "justified," these feelings still drain me of my energy. Although anger can be a driving force to become clear and set up boundaries towards others, it is still very exhausting. I have become aware that when I scan my life to find out what is missing, I first need to look at the stress patterns I carry inside: to ask who or what am I blaming for my internal situation?

Exercise 4

What are the patterns of thinking and feeling you identify with?

Who or what are you blaming for your internal state?

Mentally remove all the people you hold responsible for your condition and transform only the feeling that remains by chanting Daimoku.

Our state of life is a physiological baseline

The late neuroscientist, Dr. Karl Pribram, showed that we all have so called *baselines* that define our state of life; the way we are thinking and feeling. He states that the thoughts and emotions we have on a regular basis, the ones we repeat over and over again, are based on deeply ingrained or established physiological patterns and rhythms. These are basically the neural pathways we have formed in our brain and the coherent or incoherent rhythms of our heart. When we worry a lot, for instance, we have formed distinct neural pathways in our brain which we activate whenever we worry about something. The more we activate these neural pathways, the stronger they become. These are our basic neural habit patterns. Dr. Pribram calls these patterns and rhythms the *baselines* to which we default unconsciously. They represent our state of life. Functionally speaking, the brain is a really good pattern storage and recognition system. Whenever we have a coherent heart rhythm, our positive patterns are activated. Whenever we have an incoherent heart rhythm, our negative programs are activated.

Our state of life acts like a thermostat

We might set a new intention or a goal and put all of our will power behind it. We may manifest our intention for a while, but as soon as we are distracted or momentarily forget our intention, boom; we are right back into the old, automatic ways of thinking and feeling. We have all experienced this. If you've ever set New Year's resolutions, you probably know what I mean. How long did it take before you were right back in the same, original pattern? You can think of baselines as a thermostat in your home. You set the temperature to a certain temperature, maybe 20 degrees Celsius. The thermostat controls the heating system. It strives to maintain the temperature around that set temperature point; a little bit above, a little bit below, but around that. That's the set point. Whatever you experience on the outside, the baseline is just going to do its job of maintaining that set point.

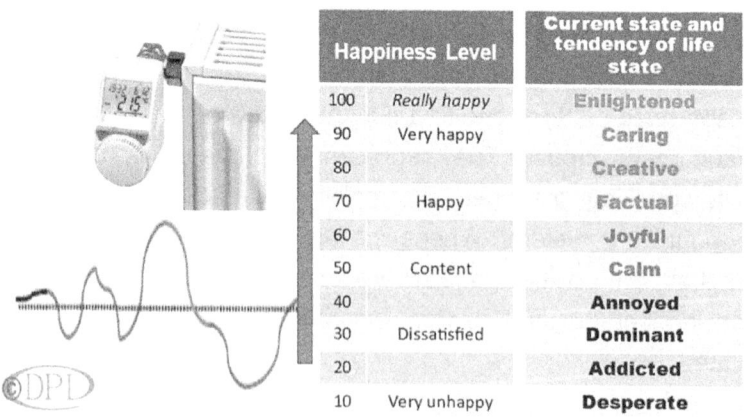

Our happiness and level corresponds to our habitual state of life (our basic mood)

Increase your happiness set point!

Happiness Level		Current state and tendency of life state
100	Really happy	Enlightened
90	Very happy	Caring
80		Creative
70	Happy	Factual
60		Joyful
50	Content	Calm
40		Annoyed
30	Dissatisfied	Dominant
20		Addicted
10	Very unhappy	Desperate

As it turns out, the brain functions very much as depicted above, across many levels. In our book »Change your brain-waves – change your karma- Nichiren Buddhism 3.1« we have already talked about the amygdala. There are two of them; one on the right side and one on the left side of the brain. Why is the amygdala so important? Well, it's clearly one of the key centers involved in creating our emotions. In creating the actual feeling and texture of an emotion: the felt part; not just the empty conceptual part.

The amygdala reacts to our heart rhythm

And now there is a surprising aspect that involves how important it is whether the rhythm of our heart is coherent or incoherent: Research shows that the core nucleus, as it's called, of the amygdala, is synchronized to the heart every time the heart beats. We have already talked about the heart sending information to the brain: There are distinct neural pathways directly to the amygdala. Every time the heart beats, the amygdala fires. The cells in the amygdala fire in unison with it. Whether the heart rhythm pattern is incoherent or coherent, this is transported directly to the amygdala.

Earlier on, we also talked about the way our emotions produce different rhythms, both coherent and incoherent. There are many different incoherent rhythms. For example, the rhythm of anxiety looks different to the rhythm of fear or frustration, and so on. All of our emotions have their own unique patterns. Those patterns that we keep feeding into the amygdala, however, become the familiar or *baseline* patterns. Those are triggered by the emotions we tend to experience on a daily basis. Thus, if you feel angry, hurt, frustrated, worried, annoyed or anxious for a period of time after losing your job; if you worry consistently about money or a friend who has betrayed you, you will become acclimatized to this feeling, and it will easily become your baseline. It soon becomes your familiar state. And this is the funny thing: your mind loves the familiar. It actually tries to go back to what is familiar because it makes you feel safe.

Our baselines are mostly formed before the age of 5. When, as a child, you watch your mom being anxious about money whenever she wants to buy something for you, you might easily form the belief that there is not enough money for you; that you live in lack. This will be the familiar baseline your mind tries to go back to when you are an adult and you will often feel lack, even if you are surrounded by abundance. However, if you train yourself to become coherent every day and feel positive emotions like love, appreciation, care, enthusiasm, abundance, joy and compassion, then you will change your baseline to a more uplifting and empowering state of life.

Exercise 5: What emotions do you keep falling back into?

Look at what is familiar to you.

_____

What feeling is familiar to you when it comes to relationships?

_____

What feeling is familiar to you when it comes to having enough money?

_____

What feeling is familiar to you when it comes to being healthy?

_____

What feeling is familiar to you when it comes to being successful?

_____

Which emotions get in the way of you manifesting a new life, a new partnership, a new career or more health?

_____

What is your baseline emotion, your basic state of life?

_____

You cannot change your baseline with your mind

Without shifting these baselines there is no such thing as sustained change in our thought patterns, in our behavior, in our emotional experience and basically in our lives. We really can't do it.

> You cannot establish a new baseline, or change one,
> without changing the inputs to the brain,
> from the heart and cardiovascular system.

You cannot think yourself into a new baseline. You have to change the patterns of your heart in order to do so. Only then, can you change the way you tend to think and feel. This is what the research of HeartMath Institute shows us. Experiencing this for myself, gave me the profound realization that Nichiren was so right when he said:

> It is the heart that is important.

I often thought that my internal situation would completely change once things on the outside had changed. But then, sooner or later, something or somebody else would trigger the same feeling within me so long as I continued a particular karmic pattern of thinking and feeling. After a while, it occurred to me that there were emotional energies inside me that would get triggered by my environment. But if I could transform them, there would be nothing left to be triggered.

This equally applies to the patterns dictating how you feel and think about yourself. Remember your heart emits a strong electromagnetic field that sends out all of your emotions and beliefs. This means that what you think and *feel about yourself* also affects how *other people* feel about you. The people around you are constantly responding to the emotional signals you are transmitting. Even if the words you use sound positive, your emotional signals may speak another language. At our core is our authentic self, the reality of what and who we really are. But, piled on top of this, is often our negative self-image that feels unworthy, guilty and full of shame. This is how we felt when we went through hurtful and negative experiences in the past. This negative self-image is often created by the early messages we received from our families. If someone in our family tells us, we are clumsy or stupid or we felt we were less worthy than others, then we still feel like this when we reach adulthood. No matter how much we have on the outside; a bigger house, a bigger car or more money, nothing will ultimately satisfy us if we do not align with our true, authentic selves. We can only transform these feelings of inadequacy by feeling the deep joy and true self-worth that comes with getting in touch with our true selves. In order to do so, however, our hearts must be coherent.

Case Study 4

> I experienced this when I realized that a friend of mine was influenced negatively by someone else who was really jealous of our friendship and tried to destroy it. That's exactly what my brother used to do. He always tried to destroy my friendships and prevent people from liking me. All the old feelings I had experienced in my past came up: the feelings

of being hurt and abandoned; of being powerless against an evil influence. I interpreted my friend's behavior as rejection.

However, my husband Yukio gave me a completely new perspective. He did not interpret the behavior of this friend as hurtful in any way, but as a complete inability to talk honestly and openly with other people. He saw that our friend had really denied his true self and was no longer aligned to his higher self: Our friend had been thrown out of alignment possessed by the negative influence of others.

I realized that I had interpreted the situation according to the old patterns of my mind. When I chanted a lot and achieved greater coherence, my heart even began to feel some compassion for this friend, because I could clearly see that he was on a path that would make him deeply unhappy. By turning to my heart, I overcame the feelings of hurt and rejection; I just felt compassion.

Ultimately, negative thought loops, fear projections, blame and resentment, generate stress hormones which continue to run through your system even when nothing external is triggering them. Often, we create the stress we experience by constantly pondering over or worrying about something. This means we can still be annoyed about something that happened 3 years ago. We can worry about outer circumstances. Do you constantly think that you cannot get a decent job because you are not qualified enough or that you cannot get the right partner because you have not reached your ideal weight? Are you making the way you look responsible for your inability to find the career, partner or success you want?

There is no true external fix for internal problems. I became aware that if I wanted to change how I perceived myself and my environment, I had to deal with my underlying patterns. If I chant when negative emotions rise up, I begin to change my internal patterns by refraining from identifying with them and instead, by identifying with the state of pure consciousness that is arising.

Whenever I switch to the state of "being" rather than "thinking" whilst chanting, that's when I free myself from my old patterns. This happens whenever I get out of my head and into my heart. And as we described in our book "Change your brainwaves, Change your karma", Daimoku is a strong pattern breaker.

According to HeartMath Institute, there is an antidote to being overwhelmed by negative emotions. Their research shows that when your heart is coherent, you feel positive emotions and your own self-image changes because you feel confidence, joy and true self-worth.

This means that by creating heart coherence, you can manage your emotions, change your mood and your perception, and increase your level of high-quality emotional energy. How you feel and how happy you are, largely depends on the rhythm of your heart.

You need Heart Coherence to change your baseline

This is where you find the key which frees you from emotions that pull you down and cost you energy. If you succeed in getting into a coherent heart rhythm, you can trigger positive emotions and restore your energy. Researchers have found that if you can change your heart rhythm to become more coherent, your brain has the opportunity to find a more appropriate positive feeling.

> Physiological coherence, in this case cardiac coherence, will result in emotional coherence.

This means that the heart plays an important role in determining your emotional experiences. By learning to shift the rhythms of the heart into a more coherent state, it is possible to establish a new inner baseline reference that allows you to choose a positive, energetic emotional state, to have access to your heart's intuitive capacities and to attain a deeper wisdom. The key to changing your state of life is in becoming coherent. The question is: how can we do this? Do we become coherent when we chant Daimoku? We tested it.

Chapter 6
Increasing Heart Coherence through chanting Daimoku

Does chanting Daimoku affect your Heart Coherence?

Since the heart is the strongest biological oscillator in the human system, the rest of the body system is pulled into entrainment with the heart's rhythms. Therefore, physiological coherence is fundamentally facilitated by cardiac coherence. As the most powerful organ, the heart can trigger the coherence in all of our other body systems, allowing us to increase our energy. Do you remember at the beginning of the last chapter when we pointed out that coherence has to do with harmony, order, rhythm and efficient use of energy?

It has always struck me that I feel so much more energized every time I chant Daimoku. Does chanting Daimoku lead to heart coherence? Well, we wanted to find this out and measured it. Did 20 minutes of Daimoku make a difference in my heart coherence?

With a HRV (Heart Rate Variability) measurement monitor, I first measured my heart coherence while concentrating and working on the computer. As it turned out, my heart coherence was somewhat low, as is usually the case when you are thinking a lot, and your mind is busy or when you are tired. A lot of thoughts were running through my head, and I wasn't really in a coherent state. Only a third of the time was my heart coherent, as you can see in the chart below.

Increasing HC through Chanting Daimoku

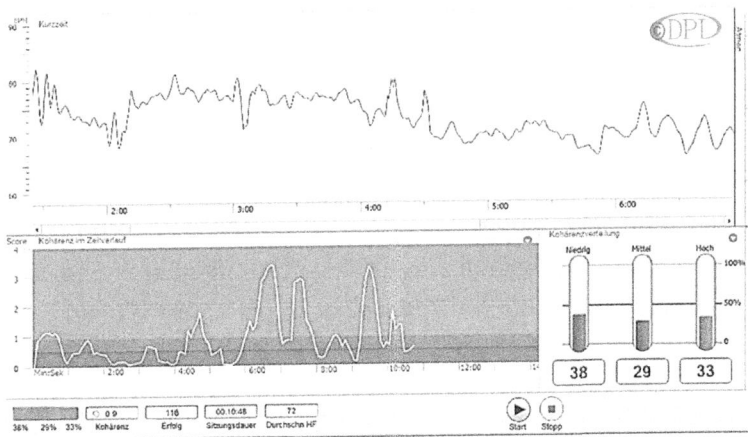

The colored bars (red, blue and green) in the picture show the percentage distribution of coherent time within the total measurement time. This means 33% of the time when I was working on the computer, my heart was in a high coherent state, 38% of the time my heart was in a low coherent state and 29% of the time my heart was in a medium coherent state.

The color red means "not coherent", the color blue means "beginning of coherence" and the color green means "coherent".

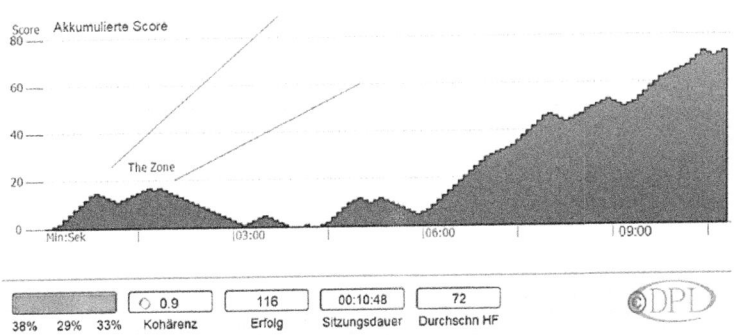

The same measurement data can be displayed as a cumulative score and this graphic also illustrates the relatively low state of heart coherence while working at the computer. As you can see in the chart below, my accumulated coherence score was at about 15 when I started. The accumulated coherence score shows you how much coherence you will accumulate over the entire session you are measuring. In the first 6 minutes, the total score remained within the range of 15 and did not increase. Only in the last 4 minutes, when I started breathing more consciously, did it settle between 40 and 70. After 10 minutes of working on the computer, it stabilized at 70. This means that during the entire 10 minutes of working on the computer, it ranged between 15 and 70.

The course of the accumulated score was unstable and often interrupted. Working on the computer was probably not the moment when the heart was truly stable and coherent. It constantly alternated between a coherent state and a moderate to non-coherent state. A busy, working mind prevents the heart from being truly coherent.

What happens when we are chanting?

Now I wanted to know what happens when I chant Daimoku for about 20 minutes. For the first two minutes I did nothing but just measure the rate of my heart coherence. Then I began to chant

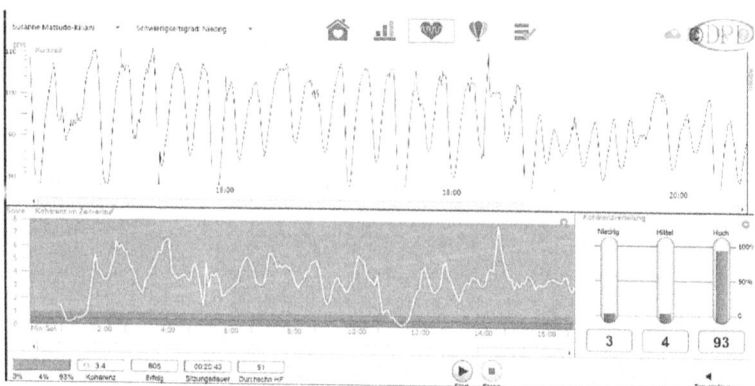

in a calm and deep manner. I tried to concentrate completely on the Mandala Gohonzon for the next 18 minutes and not get distracted. What happened? My heart coherence had improved drastically.

The colored bars in the picture above again show the percentage distribution of coherent time within the total measurement time. For 93% of the entire time, I chanted Daimoku, my heart was in a high coherent state. This ratio seems to be almost the same for the first ten minutes and can be compared with the 33% of the measurement during working on the computer. Daimoku increases heart coherence by 280%, or 2.8 times more.

Task / Coherent state in 10 minutes	Low	Medium	High
Working on the computer	38%	29%	33%
Chanting Daimoku	3%	4%	93%

What is more striking, however, is the ratio of 3% compared to the 38% occupied by the incoherent state. This means that chanting Daimoku can make your heart more than 1200% or 12 times more coherent compared to the state of your busy mind.

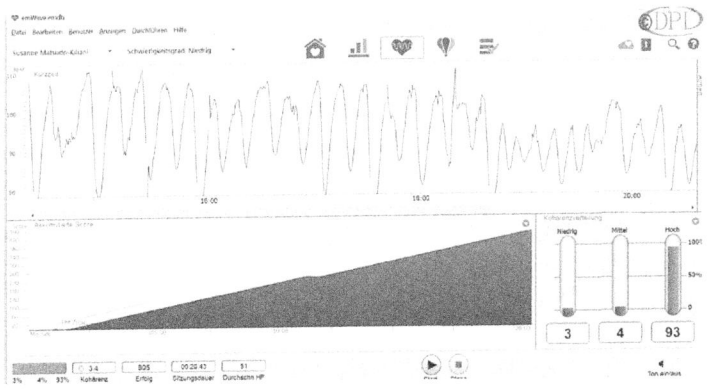

The chart above shows the rapid increase of heart coherence during 20 minutes of chanting Daimoku.

Another graph of the accumulated coherence score shows that I reached 220 in 10 minutes and 440 after 20 minutes. Compared to the score of 70 when working on the computer, 10 minutes of chanting Daimoku could produce a progressive increase in heart coherence of 300%.

What does this measurement result mean for your well-being and health?

> You can quickly and effectively improve your heart coherence through Daimoku and, as Nichiren told us,
> you will become younger and prolong your life.

Positive effects of heart coherence

Resilience increases

When we are in a coherent state, the increased physiological efficiency and alignment of the mental and emotional systems accumulates energy and therefore *resilience* throughout the body. Resilience is the ability to deal with and recover from setbacks on various levels such as on a physical, mental, emotional, and social level. Instead of falling into despair or hiding from problems using unhealthy coping strategies, resilient people can demonstrate strength in overcoming life challenges such as becoming ill, losing a job, having financial problems, going through a divorce, or the death of a loved one. They have a sense of self-confidence and emotional control to remain optimistic and calm in the face of stress and disaster. Not only are they good at problem solving, but they also maintain a solid network of supportive people they can turn to for help.

Having a high level of resilience is important not only for recovering from challenging situations but for preventing unnecessary stress reactions like frustration, impatience or anxiety that drain your energy and deplete your physical and psychological resources. Resilience is the ability to bounce back from something, to recover much quicker from all the stressful situations in your life back to a more balanced state. Now, that is true and that is one of the main benefits of resilience. But resilience is a lot more than that.

Resilience is kind of a reservoir of energy. It's our inner reserve of energy that we need to meet all the challenges we are facing every day. Resilience is also something that we can learn to increase and accumulate. So think about it this way; think about it like the gasoline in your car. When you fill up your gas tank up full, you can go a long way in your car. If there's not a lot of gas in the car, you can't go a long way. The same principle works with respect to resilience and achieving our goals. If you do not have a high level of energy, you cannot handle your problems. If you have little energy left, you might just be able to handle the problems in your partnership or in your family, but not in your job or even in society.

When we are in a coherent state, however, we live from a different zone, a different vibration, a different frequency and have the capacity to hold that frequency throughout the whole day whether our plans are going the way we want them to or whether our plans are not going the way we want them to.

Often, life and work can cause stress to mount – stress that seems beyond our ability to control. These circumstances and pressures can make us feel overwhelmed, irritated, worried and angry. They can cause our hearts to race, affect our focus, create poor sleep habits, and negatively impact our job performance and relationships. Most people try to find an external fix for this problem. They have a drink, or a cigarette. They go out for a run or just watch TV excessively. Somehow you are looking to just get a break from your own emotions. Chanting Daimoku and focusing on your heart and connecting to an empowering emotion, however, allows you to make a profound internal change. By doing so, you are fundamentally altering your body's biological baseline, shifting from anxiety, overwhelm, and stress to peace, love, and enjoyment. By focusing on your heart while chanting Daimoku, you are self-regulating your autonomous nervous system. No matter what is on the outside, you feel good on the inside. This is where the power is.

Exercise 6

Have you been worrying over finances for quite a while now, or do you feel grief over a past loss?

Do you feel frustration with a colleague?

Did someone really disappoint or betray you recently?

Do you feel guilt or shame over a past decision?

Are you annoyed about some organizational changes in your company?

Think about a situation that bothers you. Where exactly in your body can you feel the stress?

Can you feel the drain of energy these situations have caused within you?

Let's do some practical exercises to increase your resilience!

Exercise 7

Focus on your heart and imagine your breath flowing in and out through your heart.
Start to chant Daimoku and "breathe in" the Daimoku through your heart.
Do this as long as you can feel a shift in your emotions.
Connect to a renewing, elevated emotion like joy, love, appreciation or being grateful to be alive.
How do you feel now?

Coherence is not relaxation

Coherence is getting our physical systems working together in a harmonious way. However, it is essential to realize that *Coherence is not Relaxation*.

An important point is that the state of coherence is both psychologically and physiologically distinct from the state achieved through most techniques for relaxation. At the physiological level, relaxation is characterized by a shift in Autonomic Nervous System balance towards increased parasympathetic activity. Our parasympathetic nervous system is activated and at the same time our sympathetic nervous system is less active. There is a slowing of the heart rate which results in lower Heart Rate Variability. We are calm and at peace, we are going inside and our whole system seems to slow down. This is the effect of many meditation techniques.

I once took a measurement with an ECG chest strap to see how my body would react to reciting Daimoku, while I was expecting exactly that this would happen: that there would be an increase in parasympathetic activity and a reduction in sympathetic activity, as is the case with many meditation practices. However, when I received the result of the HRV measurement, I wondered why not only the parasympathetic system had increased, but also the sympathetic system had increased in the same way.

This remained a mystery to me until we started to explore the topic even deeper and took some specific HRV measurements. That's when I understood that chanting Daimoku not only calms our minds but puts our autonomic nervous system into balance. The measurements showed that both the sympathetic and the parasympathetic increased in a harmonious way and are being put into balance. Chanting Daimoku harmoniously energizes our entire body by increasing heart coherence. This to me made sense.

In many challenging situations we need a higher heart rate and *not* be relaxed. We could not perform and have the energy to face certain situations when we are deeply relaxed. When we are about to give a major presentation at work or before an important meeting with a customer or client, during an exam or before a sports event, we need to be energized, have access to all our resources and *not* be relaxed. We need all the energy available to us. We need to perform well. We need to be in top form. This happens when we reach the state of heart coherence. That's why heart coherence has become popular in sports and in the business world, enhancing our ability to function and to make good decisions. For heart coherence creates an optimal balance between parasympathetic and sympathetic nervous system activity.

> The state of heart coherence is not only a relaxed state but a state where the Parasympathetic Nervous System and the Sympathetic Nervous System are both activated and in balance. When you are in a coherent state,
> you are in a FLOW state.

The power of our beliefs

I have experienced very often that after chanting deeply in a focused manner, something that really annoyed me before or held me in it's emotional grip just simply does not bother me any more after only 10 minutes of Daimoku. I don't know any other method that allows you to transform depressing or agitating emotions to such an extent and in such a quick way.

When my favorite aunt died, I just spent the whole day in front of the Gohonzon. For what can you do if you are really depressed or upset about something? Most people tend to numb their feelings with smoking cigarettes or drinking alcohol. This, however, makes things absolutely worse. Chanting Daimoku enables you to loosen the grip of emotions that would otherwise pull you down.

Further research revealed that the electric and magnetic field emitted by the heart is not only built by our emotions, but receives its power through another significant cause, which means through our beliefs, through all the things we deeply believe in and according to which we align our lives! It is essential to feel that you deserve what you are chanting for.

Our convictions and beliefs interact with the physical world through the electric and magnetic waves that our hearts send out.

Why is this so important for us to know? Quite simply, because it makes us finally understand why some visions can easily be fulfilled, whereas other goals have not yet manifested in our lives, although we are trying so hard and visualize them while chanting. What do we have to consider in this process?

In physics, too, the principle is that if you change the electric or magnetic field in which an atom is located, you change the atom. Now the heart has the largest electromagnetic field of the body. Therefore, if we are constantly telling ourselves affirmations, or building images in our mind's eye without being *emotionally* convinced of the fulfillment of our desire or without feeling how it feels like to have achieved our goal, or without feeling that we truly deserve what we are changing for, then only our brain will send out its electromagnetic waves. But our real center of feeling, in this case our heart, then sends our real conviction out into the world, mostly our doubts and fears, with a power that is 5000 times greater. If you want more money in your life, for instance, but you constantly feel lack and worry about money or even think that "money is evil" or deep-down think that you do not deserve to have a lot of money, then it might be difficult for you to attract abundance. If you already feel abundant and appreciate all the things you already have, it is easier to attract more abundance.

If you are looking for a better job or for a loving relationship in your life but you feel inadequate inside because you are too tall, too thin, too fat, too old, too young, or simply not smart enough, then this is the message the electromagnetic field of your heart is sending to other people. The consequence is obvious: It can only really appear in our lives, what we believe from the bottom of our hearts and what we also want and feel emotionally.

> The universe can only give us what we think
> we are worthy of receiving.

If we strengthen our beliefs and already feel an uplifted emotion, the energy emitted is much greater. But when we are sad, depressed, or in an energetic hole, we can wish whatever we want: the transmitted power of the rather dismal and sad emotions that are sent out across the heart region will always be much stronger than the desire we send from our mind. That's why one important aspect while chanting is:

> Bring your desired goal from the mind level
> to the heart region.

This is exactly what my friend Sarah started to practice after she had read our books. I was very fascinated by her experience because she had drastic positive changes in her health once she managed to overcome incoherent feelings of fear and doubt when chanting Daimoku for her goals.

Case study 5

> Hello everyone, my name is Sarah and I have been practicing Nichiren Buddhism since 2010.
>
> During those years, I was able to achieve unthinkable goals, such as getting a new job or improving relationships. However, I had never thought of the Practice as a tool that could help me HEAL myself.
>
> After reading the books of Susanne and Yukio, I became less distracted and much more focused on visualizing what I really wanted, without allowing fear to creep in, and I realized that I had to keep my mind clean and not "polluted" with doubts.
>
> In 2017 I was diagnosed with Rheumatoid Arthritis, and **the doctor told me: "This is an autoimmune disease, treatable but not curable."** It was hard, I had tremendous pain that

precluded me from doing the sport I loved and worsened the quality of my life.

Well, after 6 months of chanting with a new perspective to be able to heal after I read the new innovative approach of Yukio and Susanne that showed me scientifically that Daimoku works, I went back to the biannual doctor's visit and there was such an improvement that the dosage of the medicine I take weekly has been reduced **from 15 mg to 12.5 mg**. This happened in October 2022 after years of taking the same drug.

I was really happy, I realized that I could TRANSFORM my illness! I could overturn that "sentence" of medical diagnosis and prove to modern medicine that our potential is stronger than anything!

I continued and continue to chant with this intention: on June 13, 2023, last week, I had my routine check-up and... AGAIN the dosage of the drug got lowered: **from 12.5 mg to 10.00 mg**!

Heart focus and heart breathing

But how exactly do we shift our attention to the heart region while chanting? This happens first when we focus inwardly on our hearts. We take a heart focus. How does this work? Quite simply, we direct our entire attention deliberately to our hearts.

Exercise 8: Heart Breathing

Imagine how you begin to breathe "through" your heart region. Breathe in and out slowly and deeply. Breathe a little deeper and slower as usual. As you inhale and exhale, consciously follow the slow, flowing movements.

Do you feel how your heart region slowly begins to "open"?

Here is another exercise.

Exercise 9

What would it feel like if you woke up one morning and a miracle had happened? Your life has become exactly what you wanted it to be?

Sit down, close your eyes, and imagine this scenery vividly.

What would you see?

How would you feel inside?

What changes would have happened in your career?

In your relationships?

In your health?

In your finances?

While it is a wonderful thing to be able to change your state in the moment, it is even more useful to be able to consistently feel resourceful in those situations that demand your best. Top Olympic athletes don't train for four years physically and then 'hope' they'll feel good on the day. They program their minds and bodies to 'automatically' go into a resourceful and resilient state when it matters most, in the moment of competition.

The power of coherence

Many contemporary scientists believe it is the underlying state of our physiological processes that determines the quality and stability of the feelings and emotions we experience. Coherence is the physiological state that determines our state of life. The feelings we label as positive actually reflect body states that are coherent, meaning that the regulation of our life processes becomes "efficient, free-flowing and easy," and the feelings we label as "negative", such as anger, anxiety and frustration are examples of incoherent states. But why is the state of coherence so important?

When you create this positive coherence between your heart and your brain, you're influencing your entire body and you're doing it in a positive way. These are the passive benefits of heart-brain harmony. It's an automatic trigger. You don't have to do anything more than create this kind of harmony. That's when over 1,300 positive biochemical reactions are happening in your body. You are automatically creating a stronger immune response. You're automatically triggering the release of anti-aging hormones as well as enzymes in your body without intentionally doing anything else other than creating that harmony. These are called the passive benefits of heart-brain coherence.

Whenever I feel old emotions pulling me down, I have to consciously make the decision to override those old patterns with new patterns. This requires physiological coherence. Otherwise, these old patterns keep me stuck in my old emotions and reactions. I cannot do this by logic thinking or just by logically deciding to do so. However, it takes a clear decision to do so whilst chanting. I realized I can only do this by changing my heart's rhythm and by becoming more coherent whilst chanting and by connecting to a level of consciousness that transcends my local consciousness that is stuck in those old patterns. And all this is done by the heart whilst chanting.

Again, Nichiren was right in telling us to become the master of our heart. For whenever you are in the state of anger, it is very difficult to take on a new perspective. The same applies to anxiety or fear. A coherent heart, however, gets you out of such an emotion immediately.

The power of gratitude and appreciation

Nichiren knew about the effect and necessity of positive emotions and kept pointing out the necessity to be grateful and to show appreciation. He knew that it is utterly important to be able to regulate your emotions and become the "master of your heart".

Nichiren describes three categories of people on whom our lives depend and to whom we owe gratitude. These are, in the language of his time, the sovereign, the teacher and the parent. To him, our gratitude toward our parents is essential, since it is through them that we are alive and able to exist physically in this three-dimensional reality. For Nichiren this meant repaying his gratitude towards his mother in particular. He even saw his great endeavor to propagate the law of Nam-Myo-Ho-Ren-Ge-Kyo as repaying his debt of gratitude to his mother who gave him life. Nichiren writes:

> Since I have realized that only the Lotus Sutra teaches the attainment of Buddhahood by women, and that only the Lotus is the sutra of true requital for repaying the kindness of our mother, in order to repay my debt to my mother, I have vowed to enable all women to chant the Daimoku of this sutra.

> *The Sutra of True Requital*, WND I, p.931

Thus, Nichiren knew about the power of gratitude. And again, he is backed up by modern science. For expressing gratitude and appreciation on a daily level has been linked to happiness and health. Thanking others or thanking life or the universe – gratitude in any form can make us feel happier. It even has a healing effect on us. One study shows that expressing gratitude positively affects people who are struggling with depression and anxiety, for gratitude is a natural antidepressant. The effects of gratitude, when practiced daily can be almost the same as taking a medication. It produces a feeling of long-lasting happiness and contentment, the physiological basis of which is provided for at the neurotransmitter level.

When we express gratitude and receive the same, our brain releases dopamine and serotonin, two crucial neurotransmitters responsible for our emotions, and they make us feel 'happy'. They enhance our mood immediately, making us feel good from the inside. The feeling of gratitude is also essential when it comes to putting our intentions and visions into reality.

That's why gratitude is a powerful elevated emotion that is helpful in the process of manifesting your visions and intentions because normally we feel gratitude *after* we receive something. This means when you feel gratefulness or appreciation you put yourself into the ultimate state to receive.

Exercise 10: Create heart coherence whilst chanting.

- Shift your attention to the area around your heart. Focus on the center of your chest.
- Imagine your breath is flowing in and out through that area. Breathe slowly in through your heart (to a count of five) and breathe slowly out through your heart (to a count of five).

- ➢ Now focus on the Gohonzon and start chanting. Whilst chanting send some Daimoku to the area of your heart.
- ➢ Next, try to recall when you felt good inside. Activate a genuine feeling of appreciation for someone or something in your life. This could be a special person, a pet or a place or an activity you enjoy.
- ➢ Feel this deep sense of appreciation whilst chanting. Try to sustain this feeling by keeping your heart focus whilst chanting.

How do you feel now?

Chapter 7
Fulfill your heart's desire

Create from a state of connection and wholeness

Emotion literally means, "Energy in Motion". Achieving heart coherence through chanting Daimoku allows us to economize our emotional energy in the sense that we can transform and accumulate energy at the same time.

It is only when we succeed in producing a coherent heart rhythm, that our breathing, pulse and the electromagnetic activities in our brain, work in harmony with this rhythm in our bodies. This information is then passed on to all cells of the body. The two halves of our brain are also synchronized.

Conversely, if your heart rhythm is incoherent, then it sends disordered signals to the rest of your body and to the environment outside of your body. When your heart becomes coherent, your nervous system responds by increasing your brain's energy. This has a positive effect on virtually every organ in your body. Now your heart and your brain are working together, causing you to feel more whole and connected to everything and everybody.

> When you are in such a heart-centered state
> you don't have any feelings of want or lack.

I have often heard the advice to chant as long as you feel your heart's content. This corresponds to one of the meanings of "Myō": to be "completely endowed". This is how I feel when I reach the state of heart coherence whilst chanting. I have realized that when I enter such a creative state of wholeness while chanting, what I chant for is not created from a state of lack and separation, but rather from a state of connection to cosmic consciousness. That's when I feel my "heart's content" and I am no longer waiting for something outside of me to take away the feeling of lack or frustration inside of me.

When the heart is beating incoherently, however, we feel out of balance, anxious and unfocused. Incoherence is brought on by stress which is often caused by the way we emotionally react to outside events. When our heart beats incoherently, anything in the outside world can irritate us easily. That's when we experience emotions such as resentment, anger, jealousy, impatience and frustration. However, the world looks different when our heart is coherent.

Furthermore, practicing the state of coherence creates numerous neural and biochemical events that benefit our entire body, especially our mental and emotional stability.

Heart coherence leads to mental and emotional stability.

The signals of your heart are registered by others

HeartMath research also shows that our powerful heart energy can actually impact the brains of others who come into our heart field. There are bio-electro-magnetic interactions within and between people. Did you know that even when you're not consciously or verbally communicating with others, your physiological systems are still interacting in subtle and surprising ways? Or that the electromagnetic signal produced by your heart is registered in the brain waves of people around you?

This means that by moving your heart into an open, coherent state while chanting Daimoku, you can physically impact another person. As your energy increases, their energy will synchronize with your energy. By chanting Daimoku and harnessing your heart's power, you will not only keep yourself in a coherent state but also help your partner, your friend, your colleague, or your children, to reach a positive state.

By coincidence, we discovered that we could engender 100% coherence when we were feeling love and compassion. I experienced it the other day when someone we know, Alessia from Italy, asked us to chant for her cat Zelda. She was desperate because her cat had become seriously ill with feline corona virus and it was not clear whether the cat would survive or not. We just happened to be measuring ourselves and immediately chanted for the cat. Surprisingly, I realized later that during this time, I was 100% coherent. I felt a lot of compassion for this cat, knowing how it felt to be worried about an animal you love. I wished from the bottom of my heart for the cat to recover and become healthy again. Feeling love and compassion makes us really coherent.

Chanting with love and compassion for the sick cat and its owner

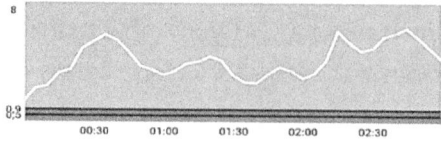

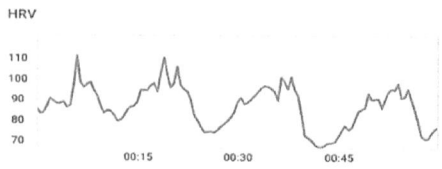

Heart coherence is essential for spiritual connection

The most important aspect of reaching the state of heart coherence while chanting, is fascinating. For the heart seems to be connected to a form of intuition that is not limited by time or space. The scientists of HeartMath Institute found something astonishing: If we manage to create a coherent heart rhythm, we have access through the heart to otherwise inaccessible levels of reality. For one thing, a coherent heart rhythm connects us to our own higher intelligence which is our true nature. However, research at the Institute also concluded that through our hearts, we are connected to a highly intelligent information field that is not bound to, or transcends, time and space.

> Have access to a non-local field of information!

> There is compelling evidence to suggest the physical heart is coupled to a field of information not bound by the classical limits of time and space. This evidence comes from a rigorous experimental study that demonstrated the heart receives and processes information about a future event before the event actually happens.
> From HeartMath Institute, *Science of the Heart: Exploring the Role of the Heart in Human Performance*

These results suggest that the heart has access to a spiritual dimension. It's the source of our deeper, intuitive guidance: our heart Intelligence; our true, authentic self. It is the true self essence of the Universe that dwells in our being, the source of all light and life within us and our true motivation for living.

> Recent research shows that there is a central relationship between the heart and spiritual experience.

This is also what Nichiren told us when he came to the conclusion that it was the heart that opened up the dimension of the "treasure tower" within.

> At the ceremony of the "Treasure Tower" chapter, the Tathagatas Tahō and Shakyamuni, the Buddhas of the ten directions, and all bodhisattvas gathered. When I ponder where this "Treasure Tower" is now, I see that *it exists in the eight-petalled lotus flower of the heart within the breast of Nichinyo*. This is like the lotus seed containing the lotus flower within it.
> *An Outline of the "Entrustment" and Other Chapters*, WND I, p.915.

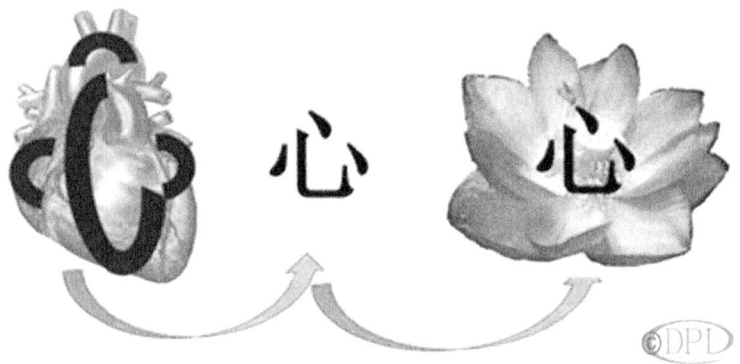

The Chinese character for heart is a hieroglyph imitating the heart organ.[32]

Nichiren compares the shape of the lotus flower to the shape of the human heart. He sees the heart as an eight-petalled lotus flower. He therefore identifies the "treasure tower" with the "eight-petalled lotus flower of the heart". And indeed, we have access to this immense and precious spiritual potential by opening our hearts. Nowadays, science puts it like this: "our greatest resource is a cultivated connection with the universe".

> The ability to continually come back to (heart) coherence acts as a gateway to the *intelligence of your higher self* and brings your energetic self into balance with your mind-body physical system. *Rollin McCraty*, HeartMath Institute

Thus, the heart is the bridge between the world where there is an infinite number of dimensions and this three-dimensional world that we live in. When your heart is coherent and you are connected to a highly intelligent information field, you no longer move through space to experience time; you move through another dimension, the realm of pure consciousness. Nichiren tells us we are bodhisattvas of the earth. This means we are multi-dimensional beings and not, as we have always been told, linear beings living a linear life which is restricted to this three-dimensional world. However, it requires heart coherence to enter this spiritual dimension beyond time and space.

We are cosmic humans.

This means that heart frequency is like a secret key that is required for us to have the ultimate full life experience that we are here to have. Via the heart, we have the opportunity to master our life's experience in the physical dimension as human beings. This is why healing occurs: not because we are getting rid of something, but as a result of connection to our transpersonal, authentic selves. Often, we are not fully aligned to our true selves. This is when we feel emotions that drag us down.

The people around us are constantly responding to the emotional signals we are transmitting. Even if the words we use, sound positive, our emotional signals may speak another language. At our core, however, is our true authentic self; the reality of what, and who, we really are.

Piled on top of this, is often our negative self-image that feels unworthy, guilty and full of shame. This is how we feel when we have been through hurtful and negative experiences in the past. This negative self-image is often created by the early messages we received from our family. If someone in our family has told us that we are clumsy or stupid or we have been made to feel less worthy than others, then we will still feel like this when we are adults. No matter how much we have on the outside - a bigger house; a bigger car; more money - nothing will ultimately satisfy us if we cannot attain alignment with our true, authentic selves. We can transform these feelings of inadequacy by feeling the deep joy and true self-worth that comes with getting in touch with our true selves. In order to do so, however, our heart must be coherent.

The heart is a tremendous gateway into a bigger reality.

Exercise 11

Imagine how your life will be different as you live more and more from your authentic self!

What do you see differently living from your authentic self?

Which new possibilities can open up for you living from your authentic self?

We know that only positive emotions like love, compassion, joy, gratitude and appreciation, cause heart coherence and that negative emotions like frustration, anger or resentment, cause incoherent patterns in your heart. Thus, it becomes clear that "your heart needs to be pure", as Nichiren said, in order to take part in the ceremony in the air. I have realized that you need to transform your negative emotions and create elevated emotions, in order for the goals and visions you chant for, to become true. This indicates that your heart is your bridge to greater levels of awareness and energy: it serves as a connection to the unified field of cosmic consciousness. You need to be in this coherent field, for your intention to become effective. That's when you co-create from a place of wholeness and completion.

Via the heart, we are connected with a highly intelligent information field beyond time and space. Nichiren called this plane the ceremony in the air. The heart gives us access to this sea of infinite potential.

While chanting, we are opening ourselves up to capturing inspiration from this spiritual presence so that the world and all its fear, lack and limitation, no longer affect us. By creating a coherent heart rhythm, we have access to this part of ourselves: our higher self which is free of worry and fear. Our higher self is not just a part of us. It is our true self. That's where we are at home. It is where we have access to all possibilities.

This means that there is a physical, biological aspect of coherence and a metaphysical aspect. Metaphysically, it means you are in alignment with your higher self. That's when you are tapping into what's true. You are getting the right cues on what to do and how to act. You are operating in integrity.

You might ask yourself how you might create such a heart-centered awareness? It is not a thought process. It is a feeling process. The heart opens that door. You can achieve this by focusing on your heart, breathing in and out through your heart for a couple of minutes before chanting Daimoku, and then remaining focused while chanting.

Being flesh and spirit at the same time

The inner freedom in the practice of Daimoku, is to remain with your consciousness in this enlightened reality, without denying or being negatively influenced by the reality of your external circumstances. This inner change is then reflected in your outer reality. Nichiren expressed this as follows:

> Anchor your heart in the ninth consciousness as you carry out your practice in the other six senses on a daily basis.

This means you should be connected through your heart to this spiritual dimension beyond time and space, anchoring your heart's ground in the ninth consciousness and maintaining this state while carrying out your practice on the everyday level with your six senses. Nichiren also tells us to stay grounded while being connected to a spiritual dimension at the same time.

Basically, you have to be spirit and flesh at the same time.

We mentioned earlier that our heart is connected to a field of information which is not bound by the classical limits of space and time. In order to have access to this field of information, research shows that you need to be in a state of heart coherence. Thus, when Nichiren tells us to "anchor your heart's ground in the ninth consciousness", in modern terms, this means:

> Maintaining the state of heart coherence
> in your everyday life.

This requires keeping your emotions high and chanting in a way that elevates your heart's balance and coherence, in order to sustain this state for an extended period of time. This basically means that even if you are at home or working in an office, at the same time, you are connected to absolutely everything. You are connected to all potentials.

But that's just the beginning: We also need to remain in the energy of that creation—day in and day out. This is where our Daimoku practice comes into play, for we can become coherent quite quickly and then become incoherent again in the next moment. Once we are able to *sustain* a coherent state, we can surrender *the how* of how our creation will show up. In other words, we are trusting that a greater mind is organizing our creation in a way that's right for us: We can let it unfold in a new and unexpected way which may well be different to what we had previously planned or anticipated. Think about it this way: If you had known all the exact details as to what you should do, you probably would have done it already.

But the moment we start to feel frustrated, impatient, angry, or resentful, we disconnect from the 9th consciousness. This is usually because we're trying to force, control, predict or manipulate outcomes.

Becoming one with the Gohonzon

The inner freedom of Daimoku practice is to remain with one's consciousness in this actual, enlightened reality of consciousness without being negatively influenced by, or denying the reality of, the external circumstances.

When is the moment you really take part in the ceremony in the air? When is the moment you are connected to a non-local field of information beyond time and space? As mentioned before, the research of HeartMath Institute tells us that this occurs when you are able to achieve a state of heart coherence. Whenever you enter heart coherence, that's the moment you connect with the quantum field and take part in the ceremony in the air. I have measured it and have come to understand that I reach the sweet spot when I take my attention off the people and problems in my life, my cell phone or my computer. Equally, when I take my attention off time: When I don't think about the amount of time I have to chant or if I don't have something to do next. Similarly, when I'm not thinking about what happened yesterday or the week before; about the predictable future or the familiar past. When I just fall into the present moment, become one with the Gohonzon and only see the Gohonzon in front of me, that's when I quickly enter the state of heart coherence. This frees me to set a clear intention. At this level of cosmic consciousness which Nichiren describes as the 9th consciousness, there is concurrence of cause and effect. Any intention which you set when you are connected at this level, is already manifested at this level, and just takes some time to show up in this three-dimensional reality. That's when things start to change on the outside.

How to shift the material world with brain and heart coherence

In order to change your life, you need a clear vision and a clear intention of what it is that you want to achieve. Very often we are asked why it did not work; why an intention has not materialized, even though you have chanted for it so often with a clear intention? What else was needed to change reality? What is the missing link that is required to manifest a new future? Which aspect is still needed to change your reality; one that is often ignored?

And indeed, often there does seem to be a missing link. And this has to do with your intention *and* your heart. In this respect, there is an interesting experiment by the Heartmath Institute that shows how thoughts and feelings affect matter.

The Heartmath Institute carried out a series of fascinating experiments on the effect of consciousness on matter. Is there a certain mechanism that enables us to change things on the outside with consciousness alone? Is it possible to change the structure of DNA samples, for instance, by human intention alone?

In order to find out, the researchers took DNA samples from human tissue and put them into different beakers. They asked the individual participants to hold the beakers containing the DNA in their hands and to send a specific intention to the DNA they were holding.

DNA beakers: Experimental samples of DNA were exposed to human intention

One group of individuals was asked to hold the intention that the helixes of the DNA in the samples, would twist tighter (see the first sample in the picture below). Another group of individuals was asked to intend that the spirals become looser (see the second sample in the picture below). The samples were then tested to see if there was a measurable effect in the desired direction: tighter or looser.

The respective groups used only thoughts and intentions in order to influence matter. The result? The groups were unable to have any effect using intention and will alone.

Another group entered into a meditative and calm state that the researchers call "heart coherence". They produced positive emotions like love and appreciation, generating heart coherence. In this state, they held the beakers with the DNA in their hands for two minutes. The result? There was no effect on the structure of the DNA.

A third group, however, also produced positive emotions like love and appreciation, generating heart coherence *and* holding the strong intention of the DNA twist becoming tighter or looser, at the same moment. And then something really surprising happened: When they held an intention in the state of heart coherence, the structure of the DNA samples did indeed change.

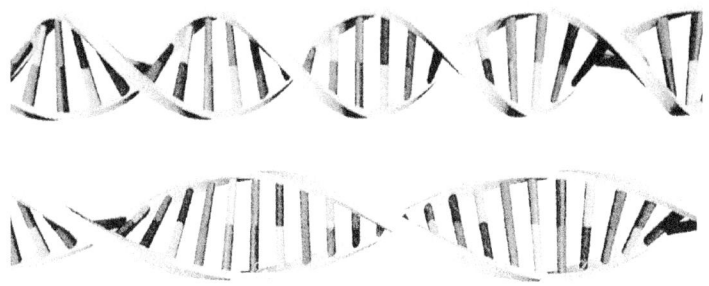

The intention was to make the spirals of the DNA tighter (sample above) or looser (sample below).

When they were later examined, the samples subjected to the intention of the DNA twist becoming tighter, were found to have a tighter twist. In some samples, the degree of twist had increased by an astonishing 25 percent; a huge effect.

When samples subjected to the intention of the DNA becoming looser were later examined, the twist was also found to have loosened substantially.

1. The clear, directed intentions and thoughts of the first group, without emotion and heart coherence, had no effect.
2. The positive, emotional state of the second group alone, could not change the structure of the DNA either.
3. Only when the participants of the third group combined a clear intention (coherent mind) *and* an elevated emotion (heart coherence) were they successful in producing the intended effects.

What are you feeling, thinking, intending, creating?
Your future depends on it!

Experience the profound joy of being

An intentional thought needs an energy source: a catalyst; a carrier. This energy is an elevated emotion. Heart and mind work together.

When you focus on your heart before and whilst chanting Daimoku, you will often experience a great joy rising up; the pure joy of being. Nichiren always pointed out the importance of joy. He stressed that chanting Daimoku was the "greatest of all joys". He knew about the power of positive emotions, telling us about the joy that arises from chanting Daimoku and the necessity of feeling appreciation and gratitude.

Referring to the passage: *"When the poor man saw the jewel, his heart was filled with great joy"* from the Lotus Sutra, Nichiren interpreted the "jewel" as the Daimoku and the Gohonzon and summarized this as follows:

> This passage refers to the great joy that one experiences when one understands for the first time that one's heart from the very beginning has been a Buddha. Nam-myoho-renge-kyo is the greatest of all joys.
> *Prophecy of Enlightenment for Five Hundred Disciples,*
> OTT, p.211

Nichiren clearly states that we will experience the greatest joy when we chant Daimoku because we can perceive that our lives are endowed with the enlightened capacity of a Buddha; free from all negative emotions. We can activate a karma-free zone in our lives to start a new life.

These elevated emotions have a higher and faster frequency than negative emotions like guilt, fear, jealously or anger. And since all frequency carries information, when we change the frequency, we change our energy. This new energy can then carry new information.

Manifest a heart-based future

> The thought sends the signal out and the feeling draws the event back to you. — *Joe Dispenza*

Thus, to manifest successfully, it is essential to combine a clear intention with an elevated emotion. A clear intention is a function of a coherent brain, which arises when you chant Daimoku. An elevated emotion arises when you produce coherence in your heart - which also happens when you chant Daimoku. The final element is to believe in a future that you are imagining or creating, while chanting with all your heart. You have to put your heart into your future, so to speak.

The formula for achieving your goals: Heart and brain coherence

---

Matching a clear intention with an elevated emotion will create measurable coherence in both your brain and your heart. This means the heart is the source which generates electromagnetic fields, connects to the unified field, and changes your life.

Think of your heart as your creative center!

Only when your thoughts and emotions are aligned and are sending the same signal, will your intentions affect the world. Your thoughts need a carrier; an energy, to be effective.

This energy comes from your emotions. If you learn to consciously create positive emotions through chanting Daimoku, you will be able to create a new future and bring your intentions into reality.

This means we need to enter a coherent state; to achieve brain and heart coherence, in order to manifest our intentions. There is lots of research which shows that people who are mentally and emotionally coherent, have the ability to shift the material world.

Fulfill your heart's desire

One of the things I love about chanting Daimoku is that desire is not your enemy. There are various spiritual traditions where desire is the arch-enemy that we have to somehow conquer, imposing on us another desire; to get rid of desire. By chanting Daimoku however, you can listen to your true heart's desire. This desire is actually a gateway to the activation of your heart's intelligence. So, the question is: What is it that you want? What's your desire? If you could have anything that you wanted, what would it be, for yourself, for your loved ones and for the world?

Exercise 12

Write down what you would really like to experience if there were no limits to what you could be, do or have. Don´t write down what you think you "should" do or what others might approve of, but only what is your true heart´s desire. See if you can remove your resignation about what is possible truly. Impossible things become possible with the power of the heart.

_____

_____

After identifying one or two things you really want, ask yourself: if I got what I wanted, how would it make me feel? What would it give me?

If you really got what you wanted, how would it make you feel? What would it give you?

Would it give you deep love, satisfaction, freedom, peace, joy, happiness, appreciation, relief?

Write down the feeling you would have if you had what you wanted.

Connect with this feeling when you are chanting for the fulfillment of your goals and heart desire.

Coherence in chanting

You may be wondering how the principle of coherence works in chanting itself? How can I chant "coherently" to achieve my goals? Well, first of all you need a mental image of what you want to achieve. It is absolutely necessary to have a very clear idea of what you want. You cannot build something that you have not dreamt to a certain specificity.

You need a clear intention of what it is you really want. In order to direct your thoughts in a clear direction, you need brain coherence. Then your thought has a carrier.

You put your intention in the present: You need to direct your energy and become aware of what you want. Clearly state what you want and *not* what you don't want. This is how you direct your energy.

You can hold an intention for more money. You can hold an intention for physical health and wellness. You can hold an intention for loving, respecting relationships and success.

> The intention is like the steering wheel in your car: it sets the direction of where you are going, but the car goes nowhere without gas. The energy you bring in is important. Thus, the elevated emotion - the heart energy you bring in - is like the gas that makes the car drive.

How many times have you chanted for a change in your life, such as a new job, an improved financial situation, a career change or an improved relationship, but did not feel this change in your heart, or were not emotionally convinced it was possible? You may believe on the surface that you can be successful or attract a happy partnership but if you feel insecure at the same time and have a deep feeling that you are not good enough, then what you really believe about yourself, will show on the outside.

In such cases, you have been sending out an incoherent signal while chanting or throughout the day. What was the result? You remained stuck in your old state. As research from HeartMath Institute has shown, in order to shift reality, you need a coherent signal where your *thoughts and feelings* are aligned. It is important that the entire message you send to the quantum field, is coherent in this way. This primarily concerns your thoughts and feelings, but also your actions.

So, whatever your goal, if you seek to shift your emotional state by chanting Daimoku whenever you become frustrated, this is the key to building the energy, resilience and passion required to follow through and sustain your goals. Your goal may be to sleep better or to limit your stress; to achieve more fulfillment, a better relationship or better communication with other family members. You may wish to lose weight or to be more spiritually connected. Whatever you wish for, you need to keep your energy high to have your dreams come true.

Focus like a laser

You can imagine this as the difference between a flashlight and a laser. That´s what dictates how quickly and clearly your own intentions can be realized. First of all, success depends on the strength of the intention you are pursuing. The strength of your intention together with a positive feeling, creates the power to change reality.

Only when the mantra recitation represents a bundled energy that produces a coherent, beneficial vibration in our own being as well as radiating outwardly, directing this positive energy into the electromagnetic field has the power to transform reality.

Whether the energy is bundled coherently and harmoniously or not, depends essentially on your concentration. Your concentration can be compared with the focus of a lens that focuses the light radiation of the sun so that a fire can arise at the focal point.

> You need a laser-like focus.

In this context, it is also important to mention that it makes a difference whether you chant coherently or incoherently. You will achieve unsatisfactory results if you focus your energy on too many things at the same time, thus preventing you from being clearly focused on your vision.

> Focus your attention: Manifesting your goals while chanting requires your focus and attention.

Often our thoughts are scattered, which means we are sending a weak signal of what we want to the Gohonzon. It is like a radio signal that jumps between several stations, causing the message to be distorted. When you send out a strong focused intention to the Gohonzon and the reception is loud and clear, then the quantum field can hear exactly what you want and react to it.

The difference can be explained by the two different properties of light: unfocused light in all directions, such as a flashlight, for instance, emits white light of different wavelengths (frequencies) which scatters with increasing distance, and loses intensity. A laser, on the other hand, emits coherent light with a single, uniform wavelength whose sharp beam of light and intensity is maintained even with increasing distance.

The incoherent light of a light bulb

The same principle applies to a light bulb. The scattered light of a light bulb, when brought into a coherent state and bundled as laser light, has the power to cut a wall. This is absolutely impossible with the scattered energy of a light bulb which is distributed in all directions.

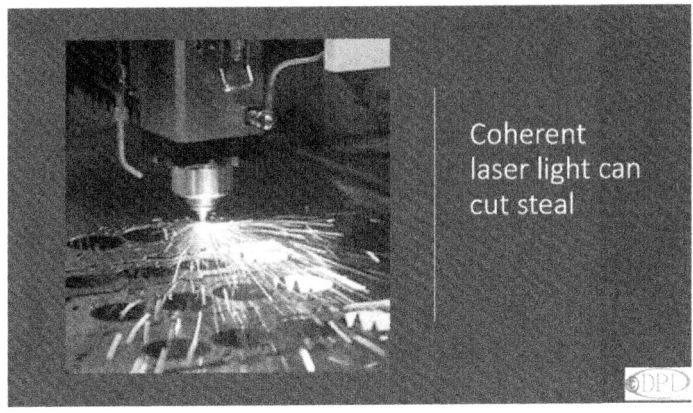

Coherent laser light can cut steal

Just imagine what a difference it makes when light is coherent or not: with the energy of a laser, you can actually cut out a sheet of steel!

It's the higher degree of coherence that has the power to make the impossible possible!

Exercise 13

Has your heart been speaking to you about the need for a change?

_____

Are you really committed to visualizing your goal?

_____

Are you adding the element of "feeling" to your visualization so that you feel it in your body as though your vision has already happened?

_____

How would you feel if your vision had become reality?

_____

Would you feel joy, gratitude, freedom, relief, some love for life?

Can you maintain an uplifting emotion like joy after chanting?

Chapter 8
Adding heart and emotion to your vision

What is your specific vision in the specific areas of your life? What is your vision in the area of health? Do you remember the observer effect? Don´t think about what you don´t want. Don´t think "I have no pain", instead put out the picture of what you *do* want in your mind, like "I have strength and vitality and stamina". No words or pictures of what you don´t want. What would you love? Be as specific as possible. You don´t just want to feel better. You want a specific frequency. You want to feel safe and confident, for instance. A specific state of being.

When you chant Daimoku, you increase your energetic state, which means your state of life, as our measurements have shown. Being healthy and happy is your highest priority. Open your heart and your energy field to the gifts of the universe and passionately desire the highest good the universe has for you while chanting.

After putting yourself in a coherent state, seek to feel and see this vision and image as vibrantly as possible. While you are chanting, once you reach the "intention point", having reached a coherent state, conjure up this specific vision of being healthy in as much detail as you can and seek to feel the uplifting energy of being in a healthy state.

Visualize health while chanting

Visualize yourself feeling vibrant, energized and healthy; walking freely and full of joy. You are in perfect health—this is what your doctor tells you. You feel full of energy and vitality. You are radiating health. You feel energized all day long. Your friends admire you and always want to know: "What are you doing to stay so healthy?" "How is it that you look so good?" Imagine what a healthy lifestyle looks like for you: Are you working out at the gym? Are you taking long walks? Practicing yoga? Eating healthy meals? Drinking healthy amounts of water? Drinking fresh juices and smoothies? Are you chanting on a regular basis? Are you getting plenty of rest? See yourself in perfect health while you are chanting. Envision yourself full of energy, moving vibrantly through your day and doing all the things you love to do. See yourself healthier than you've ever been and healthier than you ever knew you could be.

- I feel I am full of energy and vitality.
- I am radiating health.
- I can now run easily up the stairs.
- I feel energized all day long.
- I sleep well and I wake up refreshed.
- I eat a healthy diet on a daily basis.
- I establish the ideal meal plan for my body.
- I establish the ideal exercise plan for my body.

Visualize loving relationships while chanting

While you are chanting, you can imagine what it feels like to be in a loving, reliable and caring relationship. Visualize being now with the person you can fully trust. You are doing a lot of inspiring things together. You have friends and family around you; really good friends with whom you celebrate Easter and Christmas. You have friends you have a good time with: you chant together and you have nice meals together. You have a supportive network of friends and family. While chanting, visualize how it feels to feel attractive and loveable, radiating positive energy all around you.

Visualize success in your career while chanting

You really feel satisfied and fulfilled in your career. You enjoy and love what you are doing. At the same time, you are helping others. You pursue your goals with confidence and you create financial abundance for yourself and for those you love. You are investing time and energy into your career which also helps other people to get on in life. Your vocation has become a rewarding part of your life. You are working with wonderful people in a team. You have the best team you could imagine. Together, you go through deep training and transformation. You have fun together and you experience breakthroughs. You can rely on each other and trust each other. You have a strong desire to achieve even higher levels of success in the future. You feel optimistic and hopeful about your future.

Visualize abundance while chanting

You are creating abundance by creating more value for other people in your life. You have a healthy, loving relationship with money. You feel rich and abundant in all areas of your life. You know exactly how much money you want and how much you need. You see yourself living in an abundant universe. You are making more and more money every year as you are growing in your career or business. Finances do not cause stress in your life anymore and you are satisfied with your current level of abundance. You feel safe and confident. You have removed the energy of fear and limitation and you use your abundance to contribute to your family and your community. You are so grateful that you can have what you want and you love your life.

It´s never too late!

Steve and Lindsey got married in December 2022, both at what some might call an advanced age. LINDSEY, born in 1948, started practicing in the fall of 1973 in Canada and received

Gohonzon in February of 1974. STEVE, born in 1935, attended a discussion meeting in April of 1969 in the USA and received Gohonzon two days later. Because it is so encouraging, we asked them to share the experience they presented at their local district meeting.

Case study 6

> LINDSEY:
>
> Am I worthy enough to receive benefit? That is a question that often came into my mind as I have tackled obstacles over the last 48 years. I had been able to change many things in my life, one being having a successful and happy relationship.
>
> So, as I faced life alone in 2016 after being widowed, I felt I had been lucky, and that now was the time for me to forge a successful life as a single person.
>
> Between the age of 30 and 45 I had struggled at relationships until meeting my former husband in 1993. Over those 15 years I received a lot of guidance, chanted abundant Daimoku and had had success in my work and financial challenges.
>
> When, in 2019, a good friend surprised me by asking me to dinner to meet Steve, I thought I should turn up but felt very awkward about it. In my mind I was still married to my past. Also, I felt I had already achieved victory in the relationship field, and maybe that was it for this lifetime.
>
> STEVE:
>
> "*Struggled at relationships*" you say. Well, I can count six failed attempts at a committed relationship, three were actual marriages that ended in divorce. The last ended in 2010. I was single again and saw no prospect for change during the next nine years.
>
> While thinking about what I would say in this experience I realized that a process of very real change began for me in

2017 (after reading Susanne & Yukio's book NB 4.0). I decided that I believed Nichiren when he says that chanting Nam-myoho-renge-kyo immediately activates Buddhahood, whether I "felt enlightened" or not. That decision to really stop harboring doubts changed everything. The way was opened to resolve my 50 plus year complicated connection with the mother of my children, Sheryl. She moved to Portland from Los Angeles in 2012 as a family unit along with two other pioneer members. She knew I was looking for housing after I returned to LA from Northern California following my third divorce. She suggested I look in her neighborhood and in 2013 I bought my house in Southwest Portland, around the corner from hers. We were good friends, even though I had pretty much ruined our marriage with my arrogance and my lack of respect for marriage vows. Then her housemates succumbed to old age, and both passed away in 2017.

Wait, what does this have to do with Lindsey? Just that I wasn't ready to have the relationship I wanted all along until this was resolved and I had done some serious human revolution.

Sadly, Sheryl was diagnosed with lung cancer in 2017 and was seriously ill by early 2018. I was very involved in her care in that difficult time. In April of 2018 we visited our daughter who works for SGI in Tokyo, and we visited and chanted at the Hall of the Great Vow on April 20, the 50th anniversary of our wedding and the 49th anniversary of our receiving the Gohonzon. In September of that year, surrounded by family, and having communicated that she was ready to move on, Sheryl left this life.

I grieved, of course, but after a couple of months I felt freer somehow and when my old friends invited me to meet someone I had a sense of "maybe something's different."

LINDSEY:

Several weeks after we had met at a special dinner at the house of our mutual friends, the wife (who has chanted for many years) told both of us separately that she had received a "message" from Sheryl (Steve's wife who had died in 2018) that Steve and I should meet. Our mutual friend had told Sheryl before she died that she had had experience with connecting with people who had died and would be available to Sheryl if she wanted to communicate with anyone. The message she interpreted was insistent and just our two names. I (Lindsey) had only had a passing relationship with Sheryl and did not know her well. By the time we heard about this we were already established as a couple. It feels important to add this background to our experience.

As you can see by current events, life is stranger than fiction. I realized very early on after that first meeting that I had met someone who had great confidence that there was still a life to be led and wasn't afraid to venture into it.

It was his calm certainty about a positive outcome from chanting that impressed me the most in those first few days. The second realization I had was that lightning could strike twice in the relationship field, and that my fortune was truly expansive.

My practice and faith became stronger over the next few years as the world went into upheaval with Covid, and yet became synchronistic with a graceful retirement for me and joy of being isolated with a loving companion.

I think the question… "am I worthy of benefit" has become something I no longer ask. The profound and life affirming joy of sharing my life and challenging myself rather than living in a safe cocoon alone gives me an energy and freedom that I truly didn't anticipate experiencing again.

CC

Chapter 9
Global coherence

In synchrony with the universe

In our books we have frequently talked about the synchronicities that can occur when we chant Daimoku. Last century, Carl Jung wrote that a synchronicity is *"a meaningful coincidence of two or more events where something other than the probability of chance is involved."*[33] He noticed a lot of synchronicities in his own life and in the lives of his clients. In a conversation with Carl Jung about this phenomenon, Albert Einstein is supposed to have said: *"Synchronicity is God's way of remaining anonymous."*

Personally, I experienced these synchronicities more frequently after I started chanting Daimoku. When I urgently needed a job, by coincidence I met an old university friend who was working for a publishing company and who told me that the publisher was looking for someone with my qualifications. This wasn't just a job to earn money, but a meaningful and fulfilling activity, editing the entries in a new German-English dictionary. I got this opportunity exactly at the time when I was looking for such a kind of job and had been chanting for it, but it was beyond my expectation. I happened to be at the right place at the right time. I could never have arranged all of this with my own restricted, individual, local mind.

Some process greater than my mind was at work. The synchronous universe is knocking at the door of our awareness in various ways. We now know scientifically from a century of research that synchronicity happens. We know we live in a synchronous universe. But how? How does this happen?

Here's where the idea of resonance comes in: mind and matter, consciousness and form are resonating together and the resonant frequencies are going on all around us. Even our bodies and cells are resonant.

When you are joyful, you also tend to meet people who are joyful. If your joy is strong enough and you meet people who are angry or miserable, you just will not engage with them. There is no resonance there. We talked about *heart and brain coherence*. We know that when our heart and brain are coherent, they cause changes to our cells. There is resonance on all of these levels.

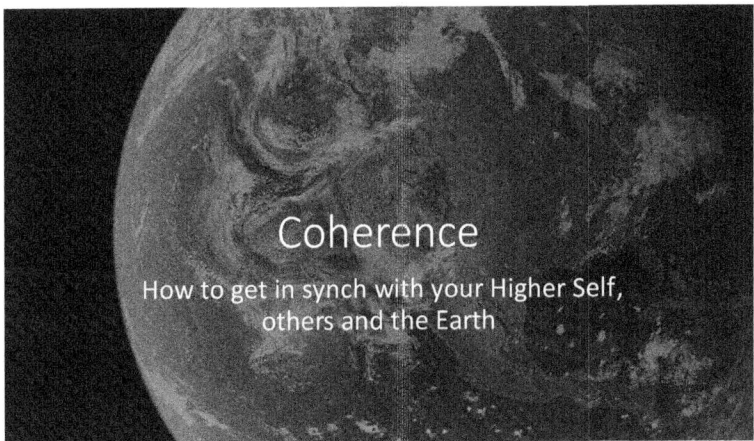

However, there is also resonance on a higher level. These resonances even scale up to the size of our planet, our solar system, our galaxy and our universe. The evidence for this is absolutely mind blowing. When your heart and your brain are coherent, you are literally in sync with the universe. As our measurements have shown, this is what happens when you chant Daimoku.

In sync with the earth's magnetic field

When we are in coherence we are also in sync with the earth. Nichiren stated clearly that anyone who chants Daimoku is a "bodhisattva of the earth." I always took this term rather metaphorically and wondered, when I found out about surprising states of resonance with the earth's magnetic field when we become coherent, whether the term "of the Earth" or "Emerging from the Earth" could also be understood more literally in the sense that chanting Daimoku puts you in sync with the magnetic forces of the earth. How come?

Did you know that the Earth is a giant magnet? Below you can see the image of the Earth, which has a North Pole and a South Pole. Just like any other magnet, it has lines of force that, in this case, radiate through space and go out for hundreds of thousands of kilometers around the planet, as you can see in the picture below.

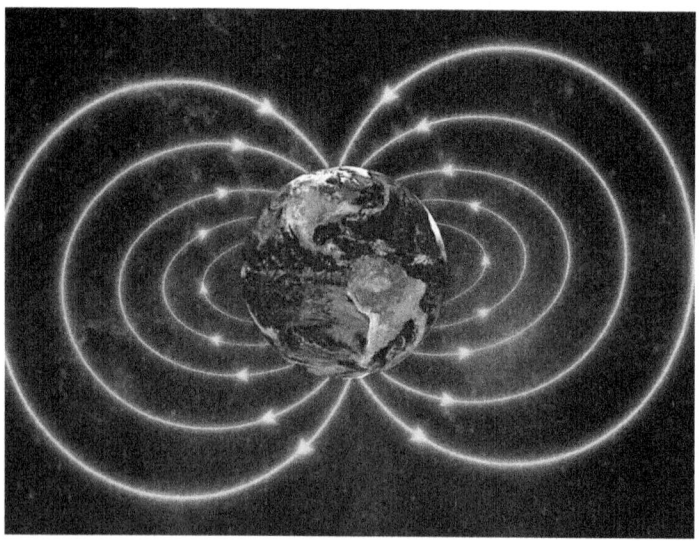

Source: The Global Coherence Initiative:
Creating a Coherent Planetary Standing Wave

The Earth's magnetic field, also known as the *geomagnetic field*, is the magnetic field that extends from Earth's interior into space, where it interacts with the solar wind, a stream of charged particles emanating from the sun.

The earth's magnetic field lines

These magnetic field lines are pushed by the solar wind. And the solar wind is driven by solar activity. The level of solar activity generally changes the speed of the solar wind moment by moment, day by day. The solar wind plucks these magnetic lines of force around the Earth like a guitar string, and this produces resonance.

Geologists were able to measure resonances in the magnetic field lines and discovered standing resonances that are always present. One of the important continuous standing resonances is the one that is always there, always at the same resonant frequency of 0.1 Hertz. Now you might ask yourself: What's so important about 0.1 Hertz or 0.1 cycles per second?

Take a look at the geomagnetic field line resonance data recorded from the Global Coherence Initiative sensor site in Boulder Creek, California. Note that all the resonant frequencies directly overlap human cardiovascular system frequencies and

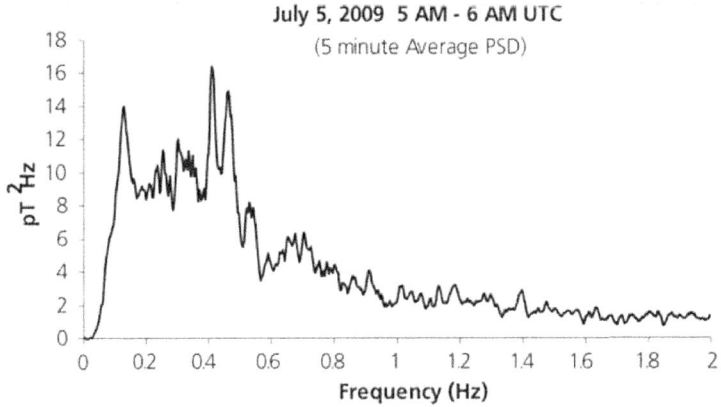

that there is a clear standing wave frequency at 0.1 Hz, the same resonant frequency of the cardiovascular systems and thus coherent heart rhythms in humans and many animals.

Well, surprisingly, that's also the frequency of your heart when you are in heart coherence. In other words: the earth's magnetic field line resonances are the same as when we are in an optimal state called coherence. We are resonating at the same frequency. We measured that when we deeply chant Daimoku, our heart is coherent at 0.1 Hz. That's when we are in sync with the earth's magnetic field.

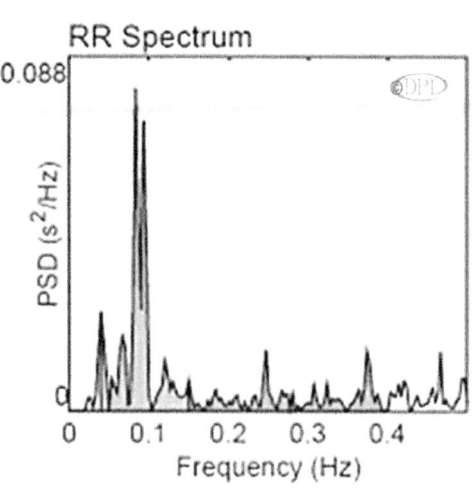

Our measurement when chanting Daimoku: you can see a distinct and strong activation of 0.1 Hz.

Just imagine this: you're sitting down in your living room, and you're chanting, and you're bringing yourself into heart coherence. Now you're in coherence, in resonance with the Earth's electromagnetic frequency of 0.1 Hertz.

How fascinating is that? You are now in resonance with the Earth. You are connected with the Earth's energetic fields. And whenever there is a resonance between two systems, there is an exchange of energy and information. When we are in resonance with the Earth's magnetic field, there must also be an exchange of energy and information between us and this field.

The Schuhmann frequency and our coherent brain

There's a second set of magnetic waves and rhythms that are also important here. These are not to be confused with the field line resonances we were talking about earlier on. This is a completely different mechanism and type of magnetic waves than the field line resonances of the Earth's electro-magnetic field. These are called Schumann resonances. They are named after Winfried Otto Schumann, the German mathematician who discovered and measured them in the early 1960s.

Schumann resonances are magnetic waves that are traveling around the surface of the Earth. Bouncing back and forth between the surface of the Earth and the bottom of what's called the ionosphere. If you're not familiar with that, think of it as a big soap bubble around the planet. There are eight Schumann resonances but 7.83 Hertz is considered the fundamental Schumann resonance.

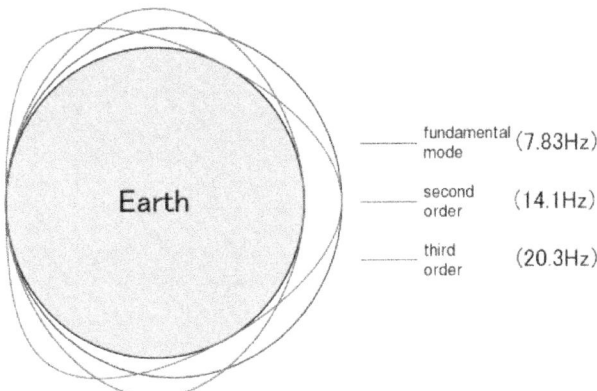

Their fundamental resonant frequency is 7.83 Hz. This means our atmosphere is constantly vibrating at a radio frequency of 7.83 Hz. It´s a repeating atmospheric heartbeat that is also known as the earth´s vibration.

It is the natural resonant frequency of the planet itself and it matches that of human consciousness at the border between the brainwave state of alpha and theta at 7.8 Hertz. The transition between the alpha state and the theta state is considered to be the neurobiological basis for the so-called "flow state". This means that the Schuhmann frequency of 7.83 Hz happens to correlate with the brain when it is in a coherent "flow state".

And this is also exactly the frequency that healers get into when they are in the healing space. When a qigong master sends energy, then he goes up to the brainwave frequency of 7.8 hertz. Part of the healing effect is to be in synchronistic resonance with the frequency of the earth and that is when healing takes place. Auditory beat simulation also shows promising results for treating anxiety by getting the brain into the Theta frequency range (4-7 Hz). This brain state has been shown to promote a feeling of overall well-being.

When we chant Daimoku, we can also get into this state. When you look at the measurement result that we showed in our book NB 3.1[34] (see below the picture "before and after chanting") you will notice that after chanting Daimoku for ten minutes, we reached a state of deep coherence in the theta brain waves range, between 4 and 8 Hertz.

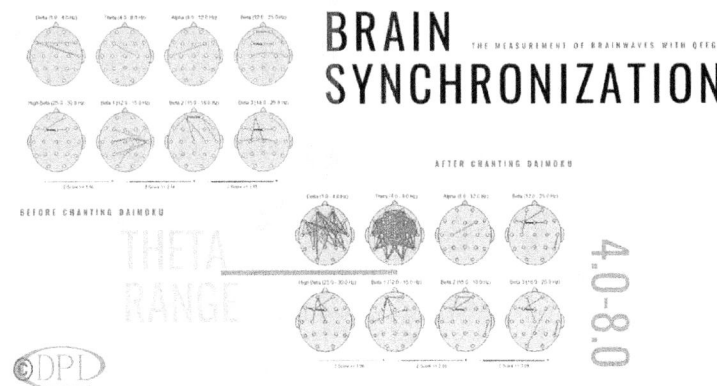

> What is really stunning here is that our hearts and our brains are vibrating at the same frequency as the Earth's two primary energetic systems when we are chanting Daimoku.

And do you remember? Two systems that vibrate at the same frequency exchange energy and information.

The meta-physical implications of heart-brain coherence

The stunning implication here is that when you are in resonance, when you're chanting, when you're in heart coherence, when you're in synchrony and when you're in a coherent flow state like that, you are in resonance with the Earth, the sun, the solar system, and the galaxy. This is our healthy state of life in resonance with the universe. So far, the coherent state of our life can be considered identical to the natural state of all beings and the universe. *This also describes the life-condition called Buddhahood. Nichiren says that chanting Daimoku **with faith in this principle** immediately causes this condition.* Based on this new insight into the interconnectedness of everything in coherence, we can gain a deeper understanding of the term *Eshōfuni*, the non-duality of ourselves and our environment. This means that we and our environment are one. We are deeply connected with the environment we are in. We reflect the environment and the environment reflects us. This is the meta-physical aspect of coherence that opens a spiritual dimension in our daily lives.

In this sense, coherence is about wholeness. It is a remembering that we are innately whole within the universe. Coherence is the natural state of the universe. Coming into coherence is the experience and embodiment of that innate wholeness which we are naturally a part of.

That's when synchronicities happen. That's when you are in the right place, at the right time and you meet the right person you need to meet in order to achieve your goals. Could be a relationship. Could be you're at the right football game or you meet the right person to get you the job you want. That's also when you get the right information you need. You are literally in sync with the universe. And you, yourself, are lifting global consciousness.

When we enter this level beyond our everyday ego consciousness, we manifest the coherent state of life. This is actually what is called "instant enlightenment".

> Chanting Daimoku means returning to the origin and
> the natural coherent state of our existence (Buddha-nature)
> and emerging from it to live and act in our daily reality
> as a Bodhisattva of the Earth.

Do we affect the earth's magnetic field?

As mentioned before, the earth is constantly bathed in electromagnetic fields. These fields affect and connect every living organism on the planet, including human beings. We are all living in a common vibrational field.

But what does it really mean to be in resonance with the earth´s magnetic field? What is the influence of the earth´s magnetic field on us humans? Does it affect our well-being, our behavior and our emotions?

Research at the HeartMath Institute suggests that the Earth´s magnetic field is a carrier of biologically relevant information that connects all living systems. It is a global information field. Studies show that the Earth's magnetic field affects us in profound ways but that we are also affecting it every day as everything is interconnected. Thus, what you are thinking and feeling does not only affect you, it basically affects everyone. This means, not only does the Earth´s magnetic field have an influence on us, but every person in turn also has an influence on this global information field. And here, the old principle of "as above so below" applies one more time. Do you remember when we were talking about the electromagnetic field of your heart and how it influences your surroundings and the people in your environment? We said that the electromagnetic field around your heart is a carrier of information and carries and transmits your emotions and your beliefs and thus influences your environment.

We showed that creating a coherent field could influence another person to become coherent even if this person had been quite incoherent before. The same applies on a global scale, for HeartMath found that our collective emotions, which is to say our collective human consciousness, affects the earth´s magnetic field, the global information field.

What is significant about this electromagnetic field of the earth is that it has a toroidal shape that not only looks similar to the fields emanating from the heart of a human being but exists in very much the same frequency range as those fields of our human hearts and brains.

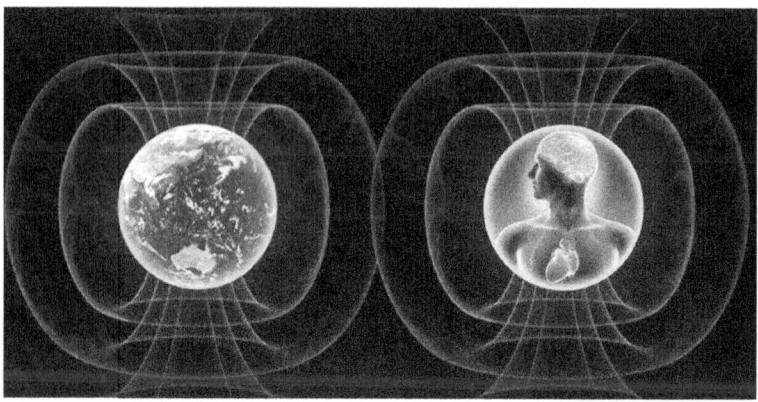

The electromagnetic field around your body is a carrier of information. Your deepest emotions and convictions are encoded in this field and thereby transmitted to the outside, affecting everybody in your environment. In the same way, every person affects the global information field, for our collective emotions, our global consciousness, affect the earth´s magnetic field which in turn also affects us.

This became obvious when NASA scientist Elizabeth Rauscher was measuring the earth´s electromagnetic field in 2001. She happened to be tracking it when 9/11 happened, the terrorist attack on the twin towers in New York.

In the picture below you can see the measurement of the geosynchronous satellite that was orbiting the earth at the time, tracking its electromagnetic field. What is striking here is that this measurement looks very much like the measurement of our heart rhythm patterns that we saw earlier, don´t you think? But this is actually the electromagnetic field of the earth being measured.

And as you can see, the measurement shows that on September 7th, 8th, 9th, and 10th 2001, the earth's electromagnetic field was fairly coherent. However, at 9:00 Eastern Time on September 11th, you see that the earth's electromagnetic field became quite incoherent and apparently remained that way for more than three weeks afterward.

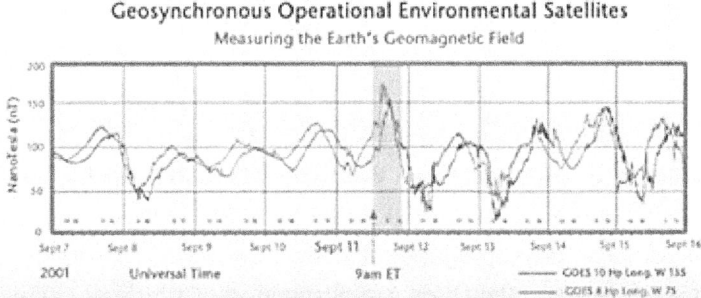

Source: HeartMath Institute

There was a collective stress wave broadcasting across the planet. And as you could see earlier in this book, exactly as the measurement of my heart rhythm shows a very incoherent, jagged pattern when I am tired or when I feel stressful emotions like anger, frustration, worry or fear, the measurement of the earth's geomagnetic field shows a very incoherent rhythm when there is a collective wave of emotions like fear, panic, anger and dismay.

I don't think anybody would disagree that these days, we also live in a pretty incoherent field environment. In recent years, there has been so much polarization and extreme separation. How do we really help feed the field with more coherence, more love, compassion and joy to help offset that discord and separation? Our measurements have shown that reciting Daimoku is a powerful way of doing exactly that. It makes us very coherent when we chant Daimoku and connect to a regenerative, renewing emotion like appreciation, love, care or joy, at the same time.

It appears as if the earth has its own "heart rhythm" which can be coherent or incoherent. The global consciousness project led by Roger Nelson from Princeton University, has also demonstrated that the collective emotions of humans can affect the electromagnetic field of the earth, but does it also affect us?

How does the earth´s magnetic field affect us?

There is a lot of research about the interactions between humans and the earth´s magnetic field environment. This research suggests that global collective behaviors and many human physiological rhythms are affected by, and even synchronized with, solar and geomagnetic activity. That´s why disruptions in the earth's magnetic fields are associated with adverse effects on health and behaviors. It has been shown that earth´s magnetic field fluctuations or distortions are associated with a higher risk of heart attacks, heart rhythm disorders, high blood pressure and breathing difficulties. It seems that when the earth´s electromagnetic field is incoherent, *we* are incoherent.

Indeed, research of the HeartMath Institute revealed that the earth´s electromagnetic field actually does have a huge influence on the human autonomic nervous system and heart rhythm.

One of the studies they carried out involved measuring the Heart Rate Variability of a group of people who were distributed all over California, for 30 days. They time-synchronized all the data from the people spread across California and calculated an average of their HRV.

What they found is indicated by the black line in the picture above. This is the HRV average together of the group. What this is showing is that these people's heart rhythms were pretty well synchronized in a slow wave rhythm.

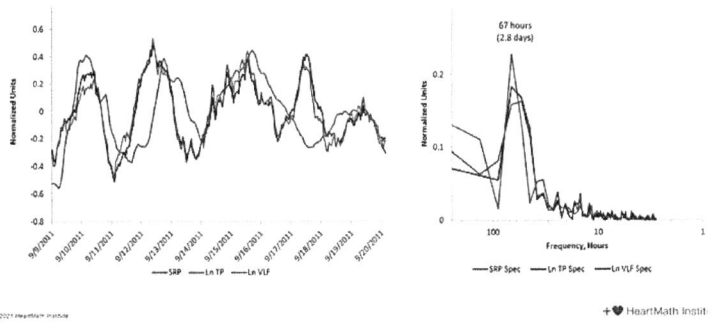

Frequency synchronization between Time varying Magnetic field and Group HRV

The average Heart Rate Variability of this group was very synchronized. And remember, one of the things that heart rate variability reflects is the activity in our nervous system; how the heart and brain are communicating. At the beginning, nobody could explain this phenomenon. The people did not know each other. How come their heart rhythms were actually synchronized? After a while it became clear that they were synchronized with each other because they were all synchronizing to a signal in the environment that we are all simultaneously exposed to; the magnetic field of the earth. That's the red line in the picture above. You can see a clear correspondence here with the average HRV of the group which is represented by the black line. Since this was a relatively small group in California, HeartMath went on to do a larger study on an international level in which they found out that reaching a heart-coherent state for just 15 minutes per day, significantly increased the synchronization of the participants with each other and with the Earth over the next 24 hours. This indicates that when we get coherent after doing a breathing exercise or after chanting Daimoku for instance, this has a carry-over effect for the next 24 hours.

In one of their recent studies, they also found out that the psychological state of the group members and the quality of the relationships between them, depended directly on how much their hearts or their respective Heart Rate Variability was synchronized with the electromagnetic field of the earth. When we are in sync with the earth, we are in sync with each other and we feel good. When we are really stressed out, however, we get out of sync, certainly with others, but also with the Earth.[35]

Collective human consciousness affects the global information field

This indicates that the earth's magnetic field can affect us in a positive way in the same way as we can affect this field in a positive way. It means that when a large number of people create heart-centered states like appreciation, care, love, compassion and joy, they generate a more coherent field environment that can benefit others and help offset and transform the current world-wide wave of fear and incoherence. We all live in a common vibrational field and each of us contributes our own positive or negative vibrations to the field, based on our thoughts, feelings and interactions. This is basically our state of life.

Our realization that not only external fields of solar and cosmic origins, but also human consciousness and emotion, can affect the mental and emotional states and consciousness of others, broadens our view of what interconnectedness means and how it can be intentionally utilized to shape the future of the world we live in. That realization implies that our attitudes, emotions and intentions matter, and that coherent, cooperative intent can have an important influence on global events and the quality of life on Earth. Our state of life matters.

When you chant Daimoku and become coherent, you are not just influencing your individual surroundings and the people around you in a positive way by establishing a coherent field in your close environment. You are also contributing to a more coherent planetary field which according to HeartMath, helps to transform the negative information caused by world-wide fear and conflict, thus helping to lift global consciousness. You are not only putting yourself in a more coherent state; you are also putting the earth´s magnetic field in a more coherent state.

Social coherence - How about your relationships?

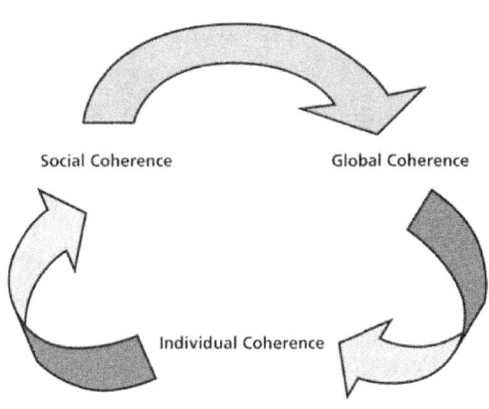

Clearly it is very important to feed ourselves with positive emotions and to lift our state of life, in order to establish personal coherence, which in turn leads to social coherence and in the end, to global coherence. I deeply realized that when my heart was coherent after chanting Daimoku, I was less reactive and I found it easier to connect to other people. Being coherent affects everything you do. As the above mentioned study showed, it also affects your relationship with other people. Suddenly you are aware of their feelings and how they feel in a certain situation that bothered you beforehand.

When your heart and your brain are coherent, this will be reflected in how you feel about yourself, how you feel about the world around you, how you treat other people and how you treat yourself. Social coherence means how you get along with others and how to connect with others. Research shows that we are communicating through our hearts with each other. In groups that have a higher positive social connection, that actually like each other, we are even seeing a heart to heart synchronization. They have this positive connection and that sense of bonding also has a non-local aspect to it. When we help others, then our wellbeing also comes into greater coherence. We are connected on a non-local level. We are all part of a unified, loving universe and yet each one of us is very unique.

When working together or just being together with other people, coherence is all about the question: "does it feel right"? Do you get up every morning with that sense of, I'm going to join those great people I work with today, and we're going to have fun because we can share our lives with each other, and we're going to get things done. That sense of getting stuff done together. Having a purpose in the team that makes sense. Having great relationships that enable you to do that.

From individual coherence to global coherence

We measured that chanting Daimoku is a very efficient and powerful way of becoming coherent and of transforming and "cleaning" our emotions. It is therefore a very efficient and powerful way of lifting global consciousness and of transforming the huge, planetary-wide wave of negativity, conflict and fear.

We all play a part in responsibility for this. There is a lot of effort at the moment in caring for the earth in terms of better environmental protection, reducing CO_2 production and the waste and garbage that is emitted into the sea, for instance. These are necessary measures to save our wonderful planet earth on the material level.

However, according to HeartMath Institute, another major aspect of the planetary shift, is realizing the need to be responsible for our own energy, thoughts, feelings and actions. In other words, to be responsible for our

We also have to clean our mental and emotional garbage!

own state of life. This, in particular, will upgrade our personal and planetary field environment. It is a responsibility like cleaning, washing up and taking the garbage out while living in our family home.

Your emotions matter

This is exactly what Nichiren pointed out. He told us that our emotions or the various life-conditions of people, have socio-political consequences and can lead to natural disasters, war and conflicts. He told us that the deeper reason for all this suffering and cruelty, had something to do with the emotions we experience in the four lower states of life.

We human beings, are deeply interconnected with our environment and what happens inside us shows itself on the outside. Nichiren tells us in other words, that all the turmoil we are experiencing right now is connected to the emotional state of people worldwide. Nichiren considers the root cause of all the catastrophes, wars and disasters we are experiencing, to be the "three poisons of greed, anger and ignorance". He tells us that war will ensue when anger and hatred are accumulated. Again, I had to think about his words when I heard about the cruel massacre carried out by Hamas terrorists in Israel on October 7th this year (2023) and the war in the Gaza area that Israel waged in response, to eliminate the power structure of Hamas. On both sides, it was the civilian population that suffered the consequences of accumulated anger and hatred. It made me deeply realize that in so many areas in this world, this vicious circle of anger and hatred needs to be transformed in order to establish peace on earth. We can all contribute to this by transforming anger and hatred in our own lives by becoming coherent when we chant Daimoku. In a modern sense, the term *"Kosenrufu"* can be interpreted as global coherence. It is something we can contribute to and increase every day, every minute and every second of our lives, by transforming our depleting emotions into renewing emotions while chanting Daimoku.

Endnotes

1. See *The Letter to the Brothers* (WND I, p.502). Nichiren quotes this sentence from the Six Pāramitās Sutra. The English translation speaks of "mind" like "Become the master of your mind rather than let your mind master you." But the original Japanese text speaks about "heart".
2. See R. McCraty, D. Tomasino: *Coherence-Building Techniques and Heart Rhythm Coherence Feedback*: New Tools for Stress Reduction, Disease Prevention and Rehabilitation, chapter 24, Springer-Verlag Italia, 2006.
3. Candace B. Pert, *Molecules of Emotion: Why You Feel the Way You Feel*, 1997.
4. For example, look at the measurement result of the immune marker IgA in the section "Enhancing the immune system" of chapter 6 in our book NB 4.0.
5. Kubzansky, L.D., et al., *Is worrying bad for your heart? A prospective study of worry and coronary heart disease in the Normative Aging Study*. Circulation, 1997. 95 (4): p. 818-824.
6. https://www.health.harvard.edu/topics/stress.
7. It is characteristic of every reformatory movement to reduce the complex teachings and practices of a religion to a single practice of "faith." With the principle of "sola fides", Martin Luther created the basis of the new gospel that one is not justified through good deeds, but only through faith. This made the mediation of salvation through the church institution unnecessary, as was the practice of forgiving sins through the acquisition of indulgences. The special status of the priesthood in relation to the laity was also abolished. Likewise, Nichiren reduced the traditional five types of practice related to the Lotus Sutra to the single practice of Daimoku chanting, claiming direct access to enlightenment for everyone. See Matsudo, Yukio: *Hairetischer Protest: Reformatorische Bewegungen im Buddhismus und Christentum*, 2018.
8. *Our Heart Brain – Little Brain in the Heart,* HeartMath Institute
9. Paul Pearsall, Gary E. R. Schwartz and Linda G. S. Russek, "*Changes in Heart Transplant Recipients That Parallel the Personalities of Their Donors*" in the Spring of 2002 issue of the Journal of Near-Death Studies in: https://digital.library.unt.edu/ark:/67531/

metadc799207/m2/ 1/high_res_d/vol20-no3-191.pdf.
10. https://www.heartmath.org/articles-of-the-heart/global-interconnectedness/each-individual-impacts-the-field-environment/.
11. https://www.heartmath.org/research/science-of-the-heart/energetic-communication/.
12. See Chapter 5 *The Buddhist deep psychology of Karma* in »Change Your Brainwaves, Change Your Karma – Nichiren Buddhism 3.1«.
13. See the section *"What is brain coherence?"* in Chapter, NB3.1, p. 79.
14. Source: Heart Rate Variability, McCraty and Singer.
15. *High Heart Rate Variability, Marker of Healthy Longevity* in: American Journal of Cardiology (ajconline.org).
16. *Exploring the Role of the Heart in Human Performance* in*:* Science of the Heart: Vol 1 (1993-2001), Heartmath Institute.
17. You can follow the development of "Top 15 deadliest diseases in the future" from 2020 until 2060 on YouTube, but there are no changes regarding the top 10.
    (2) Top 15 deadliest diseases in the future /until 2060/ - YouTube
18. *Heart-rate variability: A biomarker to study the influence of nutrition on physiological and psychological health?* in: researchgate.net.
19. Yoshioka and Terasaki, 1994, Gottsäter et al., 2006 and Kemp et al., 2014.
20. Martin Siepmann, Kerstin Weidner, Katja Petrowski Timo Siepmann: *Heart Rate Variability: A Measure of Cardiovascular Health and Possible Therapeutic Target in dysautonomic mental and neurological disorders* | SpringerLink
21. *Heart rate variability and inflammation: A meta-analysis of human studies* - ScienceDirect.
22. Marijke De Couck, Boris Mravec and Yori Gidron, *You may need the vagus nerve to understand pathophysiology and to treat diseases*. Clinical Science (2012) 122, 323–328)

    Li Xiong and Thomas W.H. Leung: *Autonomic dysfunction in neurological disorders* - PMC (nih.gov)

    J. T. Korpelainen 1, K.A. Sotaniemi, V. V. Myllylä: *Autonomic nervous system disorders in stroke* - PubMed (nih.gov)
23. Milan T. Makale, Santosh Kesari, Wolfgang Wrasidlo: *The autonomic nervous system and cancer* - ScienceDirect.
24. Mazurak N, Seredyuk N, Sauer H, Teufel M, Enck P. *Heart rate variability in the irritable bowel syndrome: a review of the literature*.

Neurogastroenterol Motil. 2012;24(3):206–216. [PubMed].

25 Thayer JF, Ahs F, Fredrikson M, Sollers JJ, Wager TD. *A meta-analysis of heart rate variability and neuroimaging studies: implications for heart rate variability as a marker of stress and health*. Neuroscience and Biobehavioral Reviews 36 (2012): 747–756.

26 Berntson GG, Bigger JT, Jr, Eckberg DL, et al. *Heart rate variability: origins, methods, and interpretive caveats*. Psychophysiology. 1997;34(6):623–648. [PubMed] [Google Scholar] [Ref list])

27 Lohninger, Alfred: *Herzratenvariabilität, Das HRV Praxis Lehrbuch*, facultas, 2. Edition, 2021.

28 To collect data, there are several different devices, but we applied a simple ear sensor with the model *emWave Pro* of the HeartMath Institute, which uses low-power LED light to measure changes in blood volume in the earlobe with each heartbeat. From this signal, the inter-beat interval is calculated in milliseconds. We then used this data to determine the HRV-specific values using the Kubios Standard software.

29 Lohninger, Alfred: Herzratenvariabilität, *Das HRV Praxis-Lehrbuch*, S. 246.

30 Zhou H, Dai Z, Hua L, Jiang H, Tian S, Han Y, et al. (2020-01-22): *Decreased Task-Related HRV Is Associated With Inhibitory Dysfunction Through Functional Inter-Region Connectivity of PFC in Major Depressive Disorder*: Frontiers in Psychiatry. 10: 989.

31 Rollin, McCraty: *The Appreciative Heart: The Psychophysiology of Appreciation* (researchgate.net).

32 see chapter 7 of NB4.1.

33 Jung, Carl Gustav, *Synchronicity: An Acausal Connecting Principle* (1952, English translation 1973).

34 See the pictures at page 76 and 78 in chapter 5, Shift your brainwave frequency with Daimoku in »Change your Brainwaves, Change your Karma: Nichiren Buddhism 3.1«

35 *Global Study of Human Heart Rhythm Synchronization with the Earth's Time Varying Magnetic Field* (mdpi.com)).

About the authors

Susanne Matsudo-Kiliani, PhD

University degree as a translator for English and Spanish, PhD in translation studies and religious studies with a focus on Buddhism, Heidelberg University. Certified trainer for Intercultural Competence in International Business.

Dr. Matsudo-Kiliani has been practicing Nichiren Buddhism since 1998 and has experienced many beneficial transformations in her life.

From 2014 to 2017 she was a member of the council of the German Buddhist Union (DBU e. V.) and acted as a representative for interreligious dialogue at the federal level for a better mutual understanding of different religions.

As a passionate practitioner she has been engaged in building a bridge between Buddhist practice and modern science that are now integrating energy and consciousness.

Yukio Matsudo, PhD

PhD in Philosophy and post-doc qualification for professorship (Habilitation) in the subjects of Japanese Buddhism and Comparative Religions at the University of Heidelberg

After receiving his post-doc qualification, he taught as a lecturer at the University of Heidelberg from 2001 to 2011.

Dr. Matsudo has been practicing Nichiren Buddhism intensively since 1976 and has supported hundreds of people in their practice and was also able to gain many concrete and important experiences.

Dr. Matsudo was active as Research Director at *the European Centre of the Institute of Oriental Philosophy* (IOP) in Taplow Court, UK, from 1991 to 2001, adopting a modern, humanistic and open-minded approach to overcome traditional dogmatic doctrines. He published several books and articles in Japanese, German and English.

Dr. Susanne Matsudo-Kiliani and Dr. Yukio Matsudo are working to bridge the gap between Buddhism, Western philosophy and new scientific approaches to present Nichiren Buddhism as a spiritual teaching and practice for the 21st century. Since 2013, they have begun to scientifically investigate the effects of the practice of Daimoku chanting. In this context, they have started many research projects, which they report on in their books.

Our publications in English

NB 2.0 *The Instant Enlightenment of Ordinary People: Nichiren Buddhism 2.0 for the 21st Century* (June 2018)

NB 2.1 *Seven Steps to Success in Practicing Daimoku: Nichiren Buddhism 2.1* (-)

NB 3.0 *Transform your Energy – Change your Life: Nichiren Buddhism 3.0* (June 2016)

NB 3.1 *Change your Brainwaves, Change your Karma: Nichiren Buddhism 3.1* (August 2017)

NB 4.0 *Focus your Mind – Light up your Life: Nichiren Buddhism 4.0* (September 2020)

NB 4.1 *Emotions Matter – Your Positive Jump Start: Nichiren Buddhism 4.1* (-)

NB 4.2 *Open your heart, Manifest your dreams: Nichiren Buddhism 4.2* (December 2023)

We would appreciate your kind support in promoting our books by writing a customer review on Amazon.book and posting or sharing our book information.

Printed in Great Britain
by Amazon